WEBINARS with WOW factor
2nd Edition

by Becky Pike Pluth, M.Ed., CSP
foreword by Elaine Biech

Dedication

To Raegan, Brody, Gabe, and Lucas

Whose sweet "I love yous" keep me going even when I'm tired and ready to be done, and you are just getting started. Because of you, I have many not-so-tiny fingerprints on my computer screen and heart.

Thank you for "helping" mommy with her book and previewing pictures. Your votes count the most.

Thank you for coming into my office and sharing your sunny smiles a hundred times and asking if my book is done yet so I can come and play or put you to bed and pray.

This may not be the best bedtime reading, but your smiles make me feel like it is. You humble me. I love you beyond measure.

Endorsements

"It's no secret that virtual training is here to stay—and so is the challenge of keeping digital learners engaged. This is a perfect time for the second edition of *Webinars with WOW Factor* by Becky Pluth, a trailblazer in interactive online training. The book offers practical assistance for design and delivery of invigorating webinars that emphasize learner engagement, retention, and application. With hundreds of tips and 44 detailed interactive designs, this book is one that trainers will keep handy as a reference for years!"

Ken Blanchard
coauthor of The New One Minute Manager® and Leading at a Higher Level

As our workforce is distributed, our learning and training must also go virtual. Becky's book provides the tools to design and deliver webinars the right way–interactive, creative, and engaging. Using these tools, you can match the learning that takes place in an instructor-led, participant-centered classroom.

Elliott Masie
Chair, Learning CONSORTIUM

If you've ever wondered how to create an effective online learning experience, *Webinars with Wow Factor* will be a great resource for you.

Maurice Heiblum
President, Elluminate, Inc.

I thought your book was wonderful! I will definitely be using some of your tips and tricks in my work. There were so many times throughout reading that I thought, "Exactly!" or "Hmmm. Do I do that?" or "Oh, boy! We better start doing that!" Thank you for making me think deeper about what I do on a daily basis.

Heather Clevenger
Webinar and Partner Marketing Manager
Elluminate, Inc.

Webinars with WoW Factor:
Tips, Tricks and Interactive Activities for Virtual Training, 2nd Edition
© copyright 2021 by Becky Pike Pluth, M.Ed., CSP. All rights reserved.

All rights reserved
No part of this book may be reproduced, stored or transmitted in any form by any means: electronic, mechanical, photography, photocopying, recording, scanning, translating into other languages or otherwise without prior written permission from the publisher, except to quote brief passages by a reviewer for critical reviews or articles. For reprint permission, contact the publisher at helpdesk@bobpikegroup.com.

Trademarks
Many of the designations used by manufacturers and sellers to distinguish their products are claimed as trademarks. Where those designations occur in this book, and Creative Training Productions LLC was aware of a trademark claim, the designations appear as requested by the owner of the trademark. All other product names and services identified throughout this book are used in editorial fashion only and for the benefit of such companies with no intention of infringement of the trademark. No such use, or the use of any trade name, is intended to convey endorsement or other affiliation with this book.

No Liability
The publisher and author hold no liability for any instruction in this book or software/hardware described herein which may cause loss or damage either directly or indirectly. No warranty may be created or extended.

Editorial Notation
For space considerations and ease of reading, the style guide for this book allowed for the use of "they," "them" and "their" following the use of an indefinite singular antecedent. This decision was made based upon the precedence set in classic literature and major dictionaries.

Credits
Editor: Liz Wheeler
Cover Designer: Imagewërks Marketing
Book Designer/Illustrator: Alan Pranke
ISBN 13: 978-1-953632-00-5

Table of Contents

Acknowledgements 1
Foreword 3
Introduction 7
CHAPTER ONE: Getting Started with Virtual Training 11
CHAPTER TWO: Curriculum Design for Webinars 17
CHAPTER THREE: Design Shortcuts 29
CHAPTER FOUR: Choosing Technology 37
CHAPTER FIVE: Training Platform Tool Overview 41
CHAPTER SIX: PowerPoint Slide Design for Webinars 51
CHAPTER SEVEN: Polling—The Webinar Multi-Tool 61
CHAPTER EIGHT: Participant Handouts—A Trainer's Secret Weapon ... 65
CHAPTER NINE: Secrets of a Powerful Presentation 67
CHAPTER TEN: Stage Presence 81
CHAPTER ELEVEN: Deadly Sins of Webinars 87
CHAPTER TWELVE: Types of Interactivities and How to Use Them ... 99
CHAPTER THIRTEEN: Interactivities 105

APPENDICES
Appendix A: Virtual Platforms 198
Appendix B: DOs and DON'Ts of Learning Champions 200
Appendix C: Additional Resources 201
Appendix D: Gaining Management Support for Training 205
Appendix E: Stakeholder Engagement for Learning Solution 206
Appendix F: ADDIE Model Overview for Webinars 207
Appendix G: Before, During and After Checklist 209
Appendix H: Objectives Term List 210
Appendix I: Tasks Required to Design, Produce and Deliver
       a Participant-Centered Webinar Checklist 211
Appendix J: Design Templates 215
Appendix K: Sample Evaluation Questions and Scales 218
Appendix L: Checklist for Co-Facilitation 220
Appendix M: Best Practice Back-Up Plans for Tech Failures 223
Appendix N: Synchronous Glossary 224
Index 226

Acknowledgements

Amidst the chaos of life, there is a serene oasis as I think about those who have helped me in this journey of writing what was to become my second book. To everyone who has interacted with me in a webinar over the past fourteen years and has helped refine my process, perhaps without knowing it, I thank you.

As beautiful and gentle as the pitter patter of falling rain, I express my immense gratitude to family, friends and colleagues. Here is virtual applause.

To Bob Pike, my dad, for introducing me to interactive webinars and providing me the opportunity to spread my wings and soar through the elearning sky. After working with you for several years, I look forward to continuing it and would do it again. Thank you for sharing freely and helping me grow as a trainer.

To Liz Wheeler, for once again being the best "producer" I could ask for. You gave me space when needed but also encouraged me to pick up the pace, which helped me see the end. One of these days we won't have such a tight deadline and will be able to sleep before going to press! Thank you for using your gift with words to make this book flow.

To Sara Davis, for providing candid feedback when it was least convenient for you, helping me "see" my blind spots, and making this book more logical. Thank you for showing me you care in the ways I best receive it.

To Rob Pike, for your time and presence in helping motivate me to keep at it, even when there were so many other things to get done. Thank you for noticing the daily challenges and picking up the vacuum to clear the way for me to focus.

To Kendra Gruman, for making my webinars flow seamlessly. You were always up for the challenge, even when testing out new activities, which required a lot of backend help. It takes a team, and you have been the best. Thanks for patiently waiting for the return of the Killer Bunnies. I promise you, that day is near!

To Scott Enebo, Rich Meiss, Doug McCallum, Janice Horne, Priscilla Shumway, Adrianne Roggenbuck, Betsy Allen, Rich Ragan, Kathy Dempsey, Dave Arch, Bob Pike, Susan Gillen Kotok and Mary Jergens for saying yes to working with me and sitting through online sessions and activities for trainer meetings. Yes, you too are in this book as part of my study; perhaps some of the exercises look familiar! Thank you for having fun online and putting up with me as your producer.

To my faithful editors: Liz Wheeler, Dr. Sara K. Davis, Barb Pike and Sue Gillerlain. The book is readable! Thanks for turning around pages in hours and staying up late with me, again. Alas, there is calm after the storm, and if you are reading this, the calm has arrived!

To Jody Majeres, you have once again illuminated my ideas. As for the cover, you nailed it! This is so me. I am passionate and enthusiastic about what I do with webinars, and you have graphically demonstrated that so well. Thank you, my dear friend.

To Barb Pike, my mom. Without you, this book wouldn't have been finished. You volunteered to watch my children when I had no nanny and a deadline looming. Thank you for reading over copy, like I was back in high school, challenging me to get an A.

To my best mate, who is proud of me on my worst days and astonished on my best days. You are my WOW Factor. Thank you for being my life mate and best friend. Until next time, cheers, Babe; this book is done!

To my Savior and Lord Jesus Christ, who has bestowed unto me undeserved grace and patience. You are the Rock in whom I put my trust. Thank you for rounding off my rough edges and loving me unconditionally. To God be the glory.

Foreword

Webinar Wisdom
By Elaine Biech— Author of *Skills for Career Success* and the #1 bestseller *The Art and Science of Training*

You can always count on Becky Pike Pluth for the best ideas and current tips when it comes to training design and delivery. And *Webinars with WOW Factor* is no exception! In addition, the book couldn't have arrived at a better time.

The pandemic has sparked a surge in online learning. This increased demand for webinars, elearning, and video conferencing is expected to endure long beyond the pandemic's end. While some nouveau online experts try to make webinars appear to be a recent phenomenon, the truth is that Becky has been a webinar expert and connoisseur for over a decade.

What makes a webinar successful, or as Becky says, adds the WOW factor? As in any successful business plan, webinars need a strategy, and that strategy must be based on high quality assessment practices. The assessment result leads to clear learning goals that define the content. Becky takes you through all these steps to ensure that you have a solid start.

Most importantly, however, for a webinar to be successful, you must keep participants engaged in the process and ensure that they interact with the content. And this is where Becky and this book truly excel.

The Webinar Wow Story
Every good book tells a story that is entertaining and enlightening. Becky doesn't disappoint us. A good book includes the what, who, where, when, how, and why of the story. Becky covers them all with aplomb.

What is a webinar? Becky logically starts the story at the beginning by defining what a webinar entails and how it differs from elearning, video conferencing, and mobile learning. However, you will soon find that Becky dives deep into the content of what makes a webinar successful. She does it with such ease and grace that you don't even know you are being exposed to some pretty complex concepts. For example, when she shares multiple analysis methods, she suggests incorporating information gathered through historical data or ride-alongs. Who knew?

Who may surprise you. You might be thinking, "Isn't this all about me, the trainer?" Well, no. Becky reveals the critical role of the producer and how this role keeps the trainer organized, prevents distractions, and helps to give your webinar more wow. She reminds us that the most important characters in the webinar story are the learners whom you will impact, so be sure to "put yourself in the learners' shoes." Of course, Becky considers you as the trainer too and gives a lot of advice about how to improve. The advice that resonated the most with me is to be yourself; she writes, "You need to do you."

Where is exciting and practical because you can be successful with your webinars from anywhere in the world. Becky shows you tricks to ensure that you and your learners always know where you are in the content and are never lost during your webinar. For example, she shows you easy ways to help participants locate where to find tools they'll use, where to post answers, and where to find information in a workbook. Becky covers it all from worldwide production to where to focus during your webinar.

When is definitely critical to producing a worthy webinar. Becky reminds us repeatedly about how essential it is to plan, plan, plan, saying that, "Once online, there is little forgiveness for those who don't!" She even provides you with a "Lesson Timing Tool" template to ensure you know the exact minute a topic will be taught and what materials you'll need.

How is Becky's specialty. As the icon of experience, you would expect this to be the book's highlight—and it is. If you are going to engage learners every four minutes during your webinar, you need ideas about how to do that. You'll find a chapter filled with 46 activities with catchy names such as One and Done, Heart Smart, Chart Chase, Double Trouble, and Q It Up to provide you with energizing activities for your next webinar. You'll learn a better way to conduct a Q&A, how to read your online audience, and practical online advice. There's even a compendium of resources and tools in the appendix: templates, checklists, and summaries. Becky's knowledge of webinars extends further to mastering a microphone, choosing a headset, and becoming adept at all the other details required to deliver a webinar with wow.

Becky Pike Pluth, M.Ed., CSP

Why all the fuss? Webinars are a cost-effective way to provide essential training for employees. They offer a tool for consultants to connect with their clients. The advantage, when done right, is that webinars allow participants to contribute and collaborate through conversation. Perfectly delivered webinars keep participants engaged. But these excellent webinars require planning and preparation by the facilitator. You want your participants to be wowed by the event. WOW is the difference between what your participants expect and what they experience—and experience it is! Becky is the essence of experience. This book demonstrates why you should ensure that every webinar you deliver is packed with WOW!

Storytelling gives life meaning. Becky tells the webinar story and gives it meaning for all of us who develop others. Whether you are a talent development professional, coach, trainer, consultant, teambuilder, or teacher, you'll benefit immeasurably from this book. You will not read long before Becky's enthusiasm and expertise inspire you to produce a webinar of wonder and WOW.

Create Your Own WOW

If you've met Becky, you've experienced her loving, generous, and energizing personality. You'll hear her voice—loud, clear, and impassioned—coming through the pages as you read the story of how to make webinars wow. You'll feel her sitting right beside you whispering words of encouragement in your ear saying, "Here take my hand, and I'll show you how."

Since the pandemic, a quick search will dredge up numerous new webinar experts; but if you want the *original* webinar expert—the one who's been with you since the beginning of webinars—you'll choose Becky and her latest book. Spend an hour with *Webinars with WOW Factor*; it is like having your own webinar mentor sitting with you, answering your questions and building your self-esteem. And even better—you'll hear Becky's version of the wonderful story of how to WOW with webinars.

Introduction to the Second Edition

It is extraordinary that this book was originally published over ten years ago when webinars were just making their debut.

Webinars with WOW Factor was my first book on the topic of virtual training and would be followed by a second that was only on interactivity, *CORE: Closers, Openers, Revisiters and Energizers for Webinar Training, Volume 5*. Just yesterday, I received an email from a participant who said, "I have your book at my side at all times. I don't know what I would do without it." Although some of the content in the original book is timeless, there are elements of live, online training that have changed since 2010. In the chapters to follow, you'll find new resources, materials, job-aids and templates to simplify the processes and speed of designing online training programs.

As I write this second edition, the world is grappling with COVID-19 and virtual training has become essential overnight. Teachers, trainers, speakers, subject matter experts, coaches, and presenters all moved to teaching and learning online with little time to prepare for such a massive shift. In December 2019, Zoom reported 10 million daily meeting participants. Just four months later, more than 300 million daily meeting participants were using Zoom.

As businesses are quickly adapting to new demands, it is a perfect time to update this book with tips and tactics that will make every webinar wow your audiences on platforms and technologies that didn't exist a decade ago.

I first started designing webinars in the early 2000s for Target Corporation. At that time, I just held my breath and hoped the technology would work long enough for me to share all the tips necessary so overseas vendors could use the software we were rolling out. Success to me at that time was getting everyone logged in and then lecturing because the platform didn't allow for interactivity. Bandwidth was an issue and almost every session had a hiccup or two without even utilizing tools more robust than PowerPoint sharing and text chat.

There were no textbooks for me to learn how to build and deliver webinars—it was a new delivery method learned by necessity. The first edition of this book was one of the first of any books on the topic of webinar training and the only one designed around interactivity every four minutes to increase retention and improve user experience. Asynchronous learning was trending as companies moved from face-to-face training to online universities that were mostly lecture-based or reading with very little interaction.

We learned during that time that very few people began and completed any form of online learning unless they were self-disciplined or it was required to earn a pay increase or promotion. A middle ground called synchronous training emerged and combined the benefits of online training with live instruction. Webinars became more popular than the go-at-your-own-pace pre-recorded lessons.

My first webinars were hosted on the most robust platform of the time, Elluminate, which included tools to design engagement and stream music and video five years before its competitors. Today there are hundreds of platforms for teaching synchronously and all include a variety of tools for engagement. Look at us now!

We have come a long way from the days of remote training to interactive and engaging webinars that span the globe! Although there are, at times, still connectivity issues, we have the privilege of the "online platform," and I am so excited to share these ideas with you that you may have an even greater impact.

Introduction

Imagine yourself running around your office hooking up wires then turning on your computer and waiting impatiently for it to boot. As it's loading, you grab a huge three-ring binder, your heart racing. In two hours, you will be hosting your first webinar—with worldwide participants, no less.

During the webinar, you will have only three hours to get information into the hands of 30 vendors. At the end of the "call," they should be able to use the new system your company is rolling out.

The morning flies by. You have prepared as much as you can to use the webinar platform, but very little is written on how to host a virtual training well.

With your breathing labored, you begin your webinar and slowly ease into the role. Three hours later, you have lectured and read from hundreds of branded slides. Your managers praise your successful training and applaud the amazing job done. Unbeknownst to you or your managers, however, some of the participants on the other end of the "call" spent time emailing one another, conference calling, washing dogs, ordering groceries and renewing library books. Just because you've taught it, doesn't mean they've caught it.

I have learned that lecturing with PowerPoint® on the computer not only enables inertia, it can drive people to other distractions. So I began developing interactivities I could use to keep learners engaged during online training sessions.

This book is for anyone who has ever hosted an online webinar and wondered, "Is anyone out there actually listening?"

This book is a compilation of tools I have used to prepare for webinars and best practices for great synchronous training that engages the learner in a variety of ways to increase retention and keep facilitators from wondering, "Is anybody home?"

If you haven't hosted a webinar that is interactive, know that you can be effective just by applying a few of the tips, tricks, and activities found in the following chapters. Start with the things that are easiest for you, and then, as you grow in confidence and ability, try out some of the intermediate or advanced techniques.

You can also save yourself a lot of time by purchasing the supplemental PowerPoint slides at store.bobpikegroup.com/music-and-media. The PowerPoint deck of 60 pre-made slides for use in your own training is affordably priced and will save you hours of design time.

If you have never done a webinar, check out a free one online and experience just how boring they can be, even if it is a topic you enjoy. Experience is a great teacher and having a foundation of what a webinar is will help bring to life what you read in this book.

To find a webinar, use your favorite search engine like Google, Bing or Dogpile, and search the phrase "free webinar" to find sessions you can attend. Add a topic of interest to narrow the search.

CHAPTER ONE

Getting Started with Virtual Training

What is a webinar? It is an online seminar that allows people from around the world to connect in a virtual classroom and share information via the internet. Webinars are a form of elearning because it uses a computer or mobile device as the classroom. I love Bill Horton's definition of elearning as "the use of information and computer technologies to create learning experiences."

Webinars are typically synchronous, meaning the instructor is on at the same time as the learner. One of the big benefits of webinars is the flexibility of attending the session from anywhere in the world without travelling. Some sessions utilize Voice over Internet Protocol (VoIP) which sends the instructor's voice over the internet digitally, and participants listen to the instructor through a headset plugged into their computer. Other webinars use a standard conference call connection where participants call into a conference bridge and talk over the phone.

When doing a webinar, companies need to select a platform, or virtual classroom program, to use. In Appendix A, there is a list of different platforms for training. If you are just using the virtual classroom to host a meeting and not truly for training, there are a lot of other options. However, if you are using webinars to help learners retain information, the platform selection is critical in order to allow interaction to occur in a variety of ways, just as it is in the classroom.

The platform can make the difference between a classroom with only a whiteboard and another classroom with a variety of tools like music, flip charts, LCD projectors and more. The second classroom will allow for more interactivities and a variety of learning experiences. A company called WebEx has a platform for meetings called Meeting Center and one for training called, not surprisingly, Training Center. You can compare these two to get an idea of the differences between the platforms depending on their intended use.

Elearning is the umbrella term for all courses that utilize technology to teach. Elearning can be stand-alone, or asynchronous, which can be accessed any time of the day by learners. These are self-paced and can include micro-learning lessons, which are typically under seven minutes long. The following terms all fit under elearning.

Mobile learning, or mlearning, is using tablets and mobile devices to interact with content while on the go. Thousands of apps are dedicated to teaching using just a mobile device. As a mom, I appreciate this because it has allowed our kids to bring their classrooms with us. While one son is at basketball practice, another son can be on the phone working on his "quizlet" or using Google Earth to help with a social studies project.

Gamification and learning simulations utilize the elements of game playing to tap into internal motivators for learning (friendly competition with self and others, rewards, progress, status, etc.).

Video conferencing utilizes technology to see and hear one another in different locations as though you were in the same room. This is sometimes known as a webcast. Just because you're using the technology that could be used to do virtual training does not necessarily mean what you are doing is a virtual training.

And finally, webinars. For the purpose of this book, we are defining webinars as virtual training that is done over the internet where the learner and teacher are live and online at the same time. It should be interactive and engaging and should allow for participants to connect with one another from different locations simultaneously. It is also called virtual instructor-led training (VILT). While webinars are one form of elearning, they oftentimes incorporate other types of elearning.

Webinar preparation starts with understanding what a webinar is and how it should look, sound and feel. If you haven't already participated in at least one webinar, it would be to your advantage to do so before reading further. The Bob Pike Group offers free webinars every month and models participant-centered online methodology. When elearning is participant-centered, it's more enjoyable for the learner and trainer, and this type of active learning results in dramatically higher retention and follow-through on the job. Successful webinars get people to connect, engage and learn. These online, one-hour trainings are your chance to not only learn new ideas, but be inspired and see what good looks like.

Webinar Team Members

There are three main roles in every training webinar. The first is that of the facilitator or trainer. Because I train in the classroom as well as online, I go by the latter. Whatever you choose to call yourself, be consistent. The trainer is responsible for much of the design and development and, once the session begins, is accountable for the delivery of the content.

Training online is very different from in the classroom. A rock star classroom trainer or keynoter does not automatically make a good online presenter. When teaching in a webinar, there are no smiling faces, no audible laughter, and no opportunity to ensure a learner is sitting at the computer and absorbing information. You cannot rely on watching the room to know when an engaging exercise needs to be done. It has to be pre-planned and executed with enthusiasm.

Creating an engaging learning environment online is more than just having learners text chat one another constantly or having them read from slides. It is about keeping them involved in a variety of ways—building a community where they get to know one another so they don't feel isolated. This can be done by welcoming participants as they enter the "room" and having them answer scrolling questions as others are still logging in.

As the trainer is guiding participants down the learning trail, the producer works to circumnavigate any road blocks or delays and is ready with a backup plan should technology fail.

A producer, also often called a moderator, plays many roles. When I present, I like to have my producer work through some soft opening slides prior to the event. These slides include how to use the tools on the platform and can include some fun questions to answer for those who arrive early. Our producer helps keep the timing, mutes learners, turns on/off tools, starts recording, sets timers for breaks, creates breakout rooms, pulls breakout room slides into the main room, and takes snapshots of significant slides learners have created that we then send out later. Producers also send out the follow-up emails.

The producer should have administrative rights to the session so she can fulfill platform-task responsibilities like creating breakout rooms, putting learners into those rooms, clearing whiteboards, putting up correct polling buttons, and answering text chat questions as they come in. The producer manages pretty much anything in the background so the trainer's focus can be on the content and not on the logistics. The producer can also step in as a participant if another person is needed for partners or role-plays.

The final role is that of the learner. Help create an environment that is safe and enjoyable for learners by having them come prepared. Send them a welcome letter with instructions on how to successfully log in and state specifically what the computer requirements are. When details are covered and a novice participant successfully logs in for the first time, there is a lot of motivation, positive energy, and can-do attitude a trainer can draw from. Poor planning, on the other hand, can set you so far back, you may never be able to get learners motivated again.

As you plan, put yourself in the learners' shoes and take a look at their view. Always look for times to thank them for participating and sharing, reward their involvement, and encourage them to look for ways to adapt, adopt, and apply the content back on the job. Encouragement goes a long way for participants on the other side of the monitor.

Interaction

An integral part of successful webinars is the interaction you build into them. Interaction comes in various forms. Learners might read, write in a workbook, type on the whiteboard, reflect, listen to different voices, answer a poll, or chat.

The more inexperienced the webinar audience is with the platform and the content, the more focused they are on trying to stay with the facilitator. Their distractions are typically user error and time spent with a producer trying to figure out where they are and what they are supposed to be doing.

The more advanced the user is with either the subject matter or the webinar tools, the quicker they get distracted and the more likely they are to leave their computer and run to the grocery store or do laundry!

These true stories happen because facilitators are designing synchronous training as though it was a conference call.

If participants know they are not going to be "watched" or expected to do more than listen, then they can get away with being distracted. As a solution, have designers plan for interaction from the very moment the virtual classroom opens and every 4 minutes thereafter. Use the Design Templates in Appendix J to make sure there is something engaging your learners regularly.

Create Active Learning Activities

When opening a building toy like LEGO bricks, there is usually an image of something that can be built along with the instructions. What makes LEGO bricks fun? Their flexibility—a choice of either reading the instructions or ignoring them and diving right in to create something. There is no right or wrong way of building. If there are parts left over, it just leaves more for creating another object. But what if there was only one item that could be made and each time it was done, it was created in the exact same order, piece by piece? How many times would someone enjoy the process? After the third or fourth time, it gets old.

The same is true when learning. If the same activities are repeated with little or no variation, the learner once again begins to tune out the lesson and goes back to emailing or harvesting crops on their virtual farm.

Active learning involves the learner and compels them to read, speak, listen, think deeply, write (fill-in-the-blanks and separate notes pages on the whiteboard or chat area), brainstorm, problem-solve, or even laugh.

Active learning activities go back to the teachings of Socrates. It puts learners in a position where they are the ones doing the work. They are experiencing the technology, the problem, the product. Active learning requires thinking.

A well-crafted lecture only requires low-level comprehension where a listener may write down notes, but he is left unchanged. Change is what makes an interactive webinar different. Retention is increased, and that is done through the participation of every learner on a regular basis throughout the session. So many webinars don't integrate this, which is why webinars often are attended by login only. If active learning is employed, attendance will go up as well as retention, because attendees are involved and doing.

The second half of this book provides you with ideas to get learners engaged, excited, and interested in the content being taught. By inserting your content into the activity frames, you will save yourself a lot of time!

Another great companion resource is the PowerPoint deck for these activities. These slides will save you hours of searching for just the right slide, save you the cost of purchasing the rights for use, and will spare you the tedium of attempting to create engaging slides. The companion deck is available at store.BobPikeGroup.com/music-and-media and follow the PowerPoint design principles covered in chapter 6.

Select Champions or Captains

When teaching in any setting, think about having champions of the training session. For a webinar training, these champions are the "go-to" people after the class. If it is a technical session, they may have been the pilot participants who typically have a bit more content depth, so they are able to provide support or solutions to others. If the webinar is reaching out to nine branches, there would be a champion or captain at each branch.

Champions should have a supportive attitude about the topic. In general, they are peers to the learners. This is important because learners work harder for each other. These individuals should have a positive spirit and be encouraging as well as willing to give candid feedback to the designers so that enhancements can be made. Use champions to help promote the upcoming webinars and market the training, as well as on the backend for follow-up on training issues or bridging content. DOs and DON'Ts for learning champions to think about can be found in Appendix B.

CHAPTER TWO
Curriculum Design for Webinars

Instructional Systems Design

Ken Molay, president of Webinar Success, says actual attendance for free webinars for the general public is about 33 percent of those who registered. If you target a specialized audience, attendance goes up to about 50 percent. For internal training and employee communications, you might be lucky to get as high as 80 percent of those who registered, even if the event is mandatory.

Why such high default rates? Any number of things—from technical difficulties to brain numbing litanies—can contribute to this reluctance and truancy.

Synchronous training doesn't have to be this way, but few who experienced awful elearning are excited to try it again to see how good elearning can be. If you have one shot at a great webinar, give it your all and start off right with strong design and interactivity built into it.

If you are very confident in instructional systems design, I would encourage you to at least skim the following materials as there are a lot of best practices incorporated that go beyond ISD.

There is no such thing as a perfect webinar, but there are definitely better and best practices. One of those best practices is doing your due diligence when designing the course. In my experience, most of the webinars I have seen that failed did so because of a flaw in the design process. In classroom training, this process is called instructional design (ID). For elearning, it is called instructional systems design (ISD). This book will cover, at a high-level, some of the ISD elements needed for success, but there are numerous books on the topic that will bring you deeper. (For a list of suggested books and resources, see Appendix C.)

Virtual training is a wonderful tool, but keep in mind it cannot fully replace live training. It's important to evaluate when webinars are the best approach for the task or goal. William Horton, one of the best learning design and webinar developers, said, "If you can test it online, you can teach it online." Based on that approach, video conferencing might be the best solution if you need to do a high-level rollout of a new product. A conference call might be best for weekly check-ins with your team. Step back and ask yourself if you are able to test every element online and if that is actually required. If you can't, don't make more work for yourself just because technology offers bells and whistles.

Once you have determined that live, online training is the best solution for your next training, then it is time to begin the design process. The design of the webinar will determine everything—from the hardware and software needed to the selection of materials or media used. It will also determine your budget and the timing of the course roll-out.

No matter what type of learning project you are working on, not gaining management buy-in and support before the design occurs is a common failure, and aligning learning goals and training content to business goals will help make getting that buy-in easier. When you need to ask for additional resources for online training, such as new technology or someone to act as producer, having management on board will make acquiring those assets easier.

For 10 strategies for gaining management support for your training, see Appendix D. You will also find a worksheet The Bob Pike Group uses to determine who the stakeholders are in order to determine who to approach to gain support in Appendix E. (This can be used for both virtual and classroom training.)

Results-Based Design

Results-Based Design (RBD) is an eight-step repeatable process I use for my ISD. The analysis phase of the process usually takes about 25 percent of the time. When you invest the time up front to make sure you're getting the right data, it saves time writing and re-writing a course. I use this version when I am designing a new course that is longer than three hours or converting a larger in-person class to a webinar. After having designed literally hundreds of online programs, I have found that a six-to-seven-hour in-person class becomes a three-hour online course.

If you desire to really dive into performance analysis or need great questions to help you get started, I highly recommend the book *First Things Fast* by Allison Rossett.

Results-Based Design Format Breakdown

1. Determine the purpose. I ask the following three questions:

- Why is this virtual course important?
- Why are we developing this online course?
- What business objective or goal does this webinar align with?

If you are brand new to designing webinars, you may need and want to go more in-depth than just those three. Following are some questions to help you do just that. Some of these questions fall into the other seven steps, but having them here will allow you to choose at the outset if you want those questions answered.

- Why is this course important?
- Why are we developing this course?
- What are the business challenges you are facing that makes this course important?
- If we are successful in this venture, what will your employees be doing differently or better?
- What does success look like?
- Who will be impacted by this project?
- To what extent do they need to be involved? (in class, communication, webinar)
- For what employee groups is this training intended?
- Are there secondary audiences?
- What specific behaviors do you want to observe in the participants AFTER the training?
- What behaviors support the success and lead to stated business outcomes?
- Are these different for different audiences?
- What is the mental discipline of the learners? Short or long attention span? Are they new to the content or revisiting the content?
- How will we identify that the employees are behaving the way we want them to?
- How are they applying what was taught in the program?
- Are these different for different audiences?
- Why aren't our people behaving this way now?
- What is keeping people from having the level of success we want them to have?

- What specific knowledge, skills, attitudes do our people need in order to perform the behaviors identified?
- What do the participants need to know (knowledge), do (skills), or feel (attitudes) at the conclusion of the program?
- How do we measure that our participants have learned the material?
- Will there be a test (to measure knowledge and/or attitudes), an observation (to measure skills) or some combination of both?
- What do participants already know that can be reviewed instead of re-taught?
- What prior knowledge do they need to have in order to be successful in this program?
- What deadlines do we need to be aware of?
- What design elements need a timeline to meet our deadline? (layout, design, printing, SME, legal approval)
- Will there be Alpha, Beta and/or train-the-trainer courses?
- Who else is available to help with this project?
- What other resources are available to us?
- Is there pre-existing content?
- What equipment and/or facilities will be needed?
- Who or what can support us in this project?
- Who are the SMEs?
- Who is the project leader?
- What might get in the way of our successful outcome? Can we minimize those?
- Can we eliminate any restraints now?
- What, how, and when do we need to communicate in order to ensure the success of this project?
- What are the lines of communication?
- What tools are available and who will take the lead?
- What are the projected costs for this project?
- Are the funds already budgeted?
- What authority do we have to spend the money?
- Where do we go if we need more money?

Whew—that can be a lot of hard work! When given a client project, I find that doing a thorough analysis takes a lot of time and effort but should be done. The problem with skipping the analysis phase for webinars is that there is no way to redirect or determine workarounds if you are totally missing the mark. Companies think this takes a lot of time, which it does, but how much more time and money is wasted when programs are created and rolled out and then don't work because the content was misaligned or missed the mark?

At minimum, I recommend Bob Pike's concept of analysis using non-repetitive measures. Use a few different methods to find the information you need. Do surveys and observations or do interviews and focus groups. See if coming at the suggested problem in different ways results in the same solution. Find out if the problem is really the problem. The invested time will allow you to tailor the webinar to the need-to-know information.

Most people don't even know there are other methods to use for analysis beyond surveys, observations and focus groups. Try using on-the-job observations, ride-alongs, testing and assessments, task analysis or historical data gathering for variety. At a minimum, ensure there is a need for the training class and spend quality time designing and developing the class. Once online, there is little forgiveness for lack of planning and solid ISD.

After you have determined your questions, asked them, and had them answered, you will want to take some time to sift through the data and dig into what is "Need-To-Know" versus "Nice-To-Know." Need-To-Know is the content learners will use six times in the next month or so. With webinars, you are able to teach classes closer to a roll-out date or closer to when a learner will need the information. Take advantage of this benefit of online learning.

2. Define behaviors. I ask the following three questions:

- What will your learners be doing differently or better?
- What specific behaviors will we observe in the participants AFTER the webinar?
- What behaviors will lead to the stated business outcomes?

This step will help ensure that the content is covered while we are together in a webinar versus hoping participants will learn it after. Notice that the questions are focused on the learner and their takeaways, not on the presenter. Although we may evaluate ourselves at the end of a session, the design should focus on the learner.

Each behavior falls into one of three concept areas: Knowledge, Skill, Attitude, which leads us to step three.

3. List knowledge, skills and attitudes (KSAs). I ask the following questions:

   - What do our people Need to Know, Feel and Do to perform the behaviors identified?
   - What specific knowledge, skills and attitudes should be evident at the conclusion of the webinar?

Sometimes there are several behaviors that fall into one area of KSAs, and we can clump the content together.

After every step of the process, take a few minutes to look back. Does every KSA belong to a behavior we have identified for this webinar? Does every behavior meet the business needs? If, at any point, you are unable to attach concepts to a stated goal for this training, then it should be removed. You want to avoid "scope creep," meaning it is outside of the scope and purpose of this webinar.

4. Write learning objectives. This is one of my favorite steps. It requires time to get the specific and measurable objectives just right, but it makes the designing part much easier. The only question I ask myself here is:

   - How will we measure/assess that participants have learned the material?

Those objectives should use verbs that are measurable. Verbs such as "understand," "know," and "learn" are not measurable. At the end of the webinar, how can it be assessed that one knows or understands? Objectives that can be measured will eliminate this problem.

Here is a well-written objective:

By the end of the webinar, when given a list of 10 deadly sins of synchronous training, the learner will be able to verbally share how each can be avoided.

This objective identifies the audience, the behavior, what conditions exist and to what degree the behavior will be mastered. Broken down it looks like this:

Audience—the learner
Behavior—share how each can be avoided
Condition—given a list of 10 deadly sins of synchronous training
Degree of Mastery—verbally

Objectives should be written for the learner and be evaluated during the session, not after. If it cannot be evaluated during the session, then there is no way to verify the lesson was grasped and mastered in the class to reproduce later. If someone is just learning to swim, wouldn't it be important to test and measure her ability during swim class before sending her into the ocean on her own? In the same way, your objectives should be written well before class and, like our swimmer's skill level, measured during class.

It is imperative that objectives be written before the course is created and that they are measurable. A list of verbs for creating measurable objectives can be found in Appendix H.

5. Brainstorm activities. Whooo hooo! The fun part! Finally. It may seem like it took forever to finally get to this stage where we get to insert activities that will meet the learning objectives, but at least we cap off the designing with something to look forward to!

The three questions I ask here are:

- What tools are available in my virtual platform?
- What activities could the learner do or experience in the webinar to drive them toward desired behaviors and attitudes?
- Will external applications be used during the webinar?

Before spending time designing the activities, know the capabilities of your platform before creating an activity that won't work because you don't have the right tools. In Appendix A, I provide a grid of 12 major platforms and all the tools that are available within each one. I will say that some are easier to use than others. Some platforms require a lot of time, energy and effort just to get things to work.

As you choose activities, keep in mind the experience of your audience. There are always varying levels of knowledge with the subject matter being taught as well as varying levels of experience with the technology and webinar platform. When teaching a group that has little webinar experience, choose novice-level activities. This would include some whiteboard, poll and chat exercises. The last chapter in this book is dedicated to interactive activities for webinars. If you need more than what you find here, I have collaborated with several leading experts in the field of virtual training and webinars to bring you more ideas. *SCORE 5: For Webinar Training* stands for super closers, openers, revisiters and energizers, and it focuses on the engagement part of the webinar and provides a wide variety of ideas. There are also PowerPoint slides that can be purchased to implement activities quickly.

6. Choose objectives and activities that align with business goals and content.

   - What are the best activities to support course purpose and objectives and that relate to content?

If you have followed the steps before this one, this will just be a matter of organizing what you have done and making sure that all content has been accounted for. At this point, each KSA is built into an exercise to ensure learning has occurred. To help with chunking everything you have just brainstormed and pulled together, I recommend using a template or job aid to keep track of timing and flow. In appendix J, I share templates that, when used correctly, can save a lot of time and can quickly show if too little or too much content is in a program.

7. Flow the course following the 90/20/4 principle. Participants can listen with understanding for about 90 minutes before a physical break is needed for recharging. People can listen with retention for up to 20 minutes[1], but then our brains need a mental break. Based on that, it's a good idea to chunk information in 20 minute segments and then allow time to absorb the new information. And it helps to reset learners' attention by adding variety to the lecture with interactive tools like polling, problem solving in groups, idea-generating exercises, videos, a game or practical application time every 4 minutes. Three questions will help to organize chunks of time:

   - What content is needed for participants to complete activities?
   - Which chunk of content can be taught in each 20-minute segment of time?

---

[1] Szpunar, Karl K., Samuel T. Moulton, Daniel L. Schacter. "Mind wandering and education: from the classroom to online learning." Https://doi.org/10.3389/fpsyg.2013.00495. Frontiers in Psychology, 2013. Accessed January 28, 2021.

- Which content is Need to Know versus Nice to Know?

This is where the intangible becomes tangible and your hard work comes to life, although it can be really time consuming, especially the first few times you are creating a webinar.

Before diving into creating all materials, revisit your content with the lens of Need-To-Know. It's better to push the pause button here and really take in all the content you have before developing more than necessary.

Best Practices for Identifying Need-to-Know Content
1. How does this content tie to objectives, behaviors and the identified business purpose?
2. How soon does the learner need to know or be able to do this?
3. What level of mastery is required?

Place the content into Need to Know (this will definitely be covered in class), Nice to Know (this may be covered in class as time or questions allow) and Where to Go (links to resources) categories. After brainstorming all topics and details and identifying Need-to-Know content, determine the most logical order in which to present content. This document becomes your high level flow and is the basis for your leader's guide.

8. Create all materials. The materials fall into six categories:

- Participant Guide: What should be in the participant handout that will support activities and deliver content that is a takeaway, not a throwaway?
- Leader Guide: What experience level is the facilitator at and is there enough detail for the program to be delivered as designed? (New trainers and content being transferred from classroom to online need more specific scripting: say this/do this/ask this.)
- Slide decks with interactivity
- External applications that may require application sharing
- Whiteboard slides that incorporate tools (pointer, typing, line and drawing tools)
- Evaluations

When pulling together all that needs to be designed, it can be overwhelming at first. Take six sticky notes and write one of the categories on each. Keep them on your computer or nearby as a reminder that all six of these elements need to be developed.

As you create slides to accompany your content, know that there is no right number of slides to be used. You create a slide for engagement. Some slides may be used for 10 minutes for whiteboarding while others may only be used for one as learners answer a simple poll question.

While evaluation is often the last part of the whole training process, you need to actually consider and plan your evaluation first before doing any of the actual content design. Determining what needs to be evaluated will help you and your manager know what resources will be necessary.

Evaluation forms are designed and developed earlier in ISD and help determine what level of the organization will need the training, what needs should be addressed, and what level of evaluation is required. For example, if you are training an individual, evaluation may simply be a "smile sheet" that surveys the trainee's reaction by having them answer a statement with a spectrum of answers that range from "strongly agree" to "strongly disagree."

The following image is a job aid that will help you determine how in-depth your evaluation needs to be and what form it should take.

Kirkpatrick Levels of Evaluation

Organization Level	Needs Addressed	Kirkpatrick Level
Enterprise Wide	Revenue Needs	ROI
Division	Business Needs	Impact
Individual/Job	Performance Needs	Application
Department/Individual/Job	Learning Needs	Learning
Individual	Preference Needs	Reaction

Every webinar should have an evaluation. No matter the length of the training, a simple three-question survey or poll will get participants to share their immediate reactions to the session. If I am doing a four-part webinar, I use a three-question evaluation for the first three days. On the final day, I use the same three-question evaluation for that day, and then I give a full evaluation for feedback on the course overall. This provides me with day-by-day insight versus only an overall view. I can then make changes to the right sections instead of guessing.

I use a five-point scale, and the three questions I ask are:

- How useful was the content?
- How present were you?
- How effective was the instructor?

Appendix K includes typical evaluation questions along with the type of scale used. When using different scales, make sure the scale is posted on the screen and only questions with the same scale are on the slide. Use a different slide for different scales. There is a science to surveys and people have doctorates in Survey and Usability, and there are entire books on the topic if you want to learn more.

After you have run the session at least once, it's time to compile the data you've collected through the evaluation process to determine how it went and what needs improvement. A summative evaluation can also be used to assess the participants' knowledge of the topic just covered. This is done through assessments given to the learners and then graded to identify gaps and ensure objectives were met.

The evaluation phase can be time consuming because revisions might change up to 50 percent of the original design. Expect changes, no matter how great the designer might be.

After you are done developing the materials, find some folks to join you online for a dry run so you can test out the material and make sure it works.

When creating new curriculum, there's a lot to cover, and therefore, a lot that can easily be missed. In the appendices, you'll find one titled Tasks Required to Design, Produce and Deliver a Participant-Centered Webinar Checklist (Appendix I). The checklist has a somewhat formal listing of tasks in a fairly chronological order so that nothing gets missed.

Each platform has its own unique features, so there may be a few additional aspects to think about on a case-by-case basis. This checklist may get modified if your session is being hosted for hundreds of people at one time with multiple trainers managing multiple virtual classrooms. Oftentimes, there are restrictions to platform usability in these instances, and these sessions tend to be far more rigid and more like meetings than trainings. In Appendix G, you can find a list of informal tasks to think about in each phase (before, during, and after) of the webinar.

CHAPTER THREE
Design Shortcuts

When you're in a pinch for time—perhaps a session must be converted to online in short order—there are shortcuts you can use and still produce a great webinar. In a large project, a significant amount of time should be spent on analysis; however, when you already have buy-in and know what the needs are, you can breeze by this step. That brings us to the concept of rapid design.

Rapid Design

Sometimes, a full-out assessment isn't needed, especially if it's a small project. Rapid Design is a short-cut for Results Based Design (RBD). It's not as exhaustive, and therefore may not get you optimal results, but if time is of the essence, this is an alternative. While RBD needs to be done step-by-step *and* in order, we cut Rapid Design down to two mandatory but detailed steps. In addition to these, you can choose other steps in RBD to supplement, but these two MUST be done.

- Identify the business goal or the purpose of a course.
- Determine what behaviors learners should apply back on the job and write objectives based on those behaviors. Then choose content and select activities to teach desired behaviors.

Yes, this simplifies things a lot. The Bob Pike Group has been helping people for over 40 years use both RBD and rapid design for the classroom, but it works equally well for live, online learning.

Job Aids and Templates

Anytime you're getting started designing a webinar, job aids and templates can make it easier and quicker. The templates following help us have a repeatable process that ensures we don't miss steps and that we have the best design possible from the very beginning. A friend of mine, Cindy Huggett, who is also a leader in the field of virtual learning has written a book dedicated to job aids and templates. If you want to dig deeper, you can check out her book *Virtual Training Tools and Templates: An Action Guide to Live Online Learning*.

Quick Start Analysis

The webinar training planner template is a snapshot tool that will allow you to see your webinar laid out in just two pages. It's high-level but also ensures that you've thought about the business objectives as well as the learner objectives. It is simple enough that someone who is not an instructional designer would be able to understand what the project is about. It is a bird's eye view and a quick snapshot of the training. I use this template to help design shorter webinars.

Webinar Training Planner		
Webinar Name:		
Webinar Description:		
Webinar Log Information		
Invitation Link:		
Conference Call Number:		Max Group Size:
Trainer Name:	Date:	Time Duration:
Business Objectives		Learner Objectives
Materials/Resources		
PowerPoint Name:		
Survey Name:		
Other Resources: (Audio, video, web, links, etc.)		

Trainer's Checklist

Before Webinar	During Webinar	After Webinar
☐ Upload handout	☐ Test audio, files, links	☐ Upload recording
☐ Set up registration	☐ Log on 30 minutes early	☐ Send follow-up email with survey link
☐ Send invitation to participants – Make sure they have links	☐ Run two computers for participant view	☐ Watch for assignments coming in
☐ Prepare PPT presentation	☐ Record webinar	☐ Use microlearning between classes
☐ Prepare survey	☐ Start soft opener 5 minutes prior to start time	☐ Track assignments and email those that have missing work
	☐ Engage your participants and have fun	☐ Complete any follow-up

Session Checklist

Min. Timing	CPR Chunks	Interaction Type	PPT/Materials
-0:05–0:00	Soft Opener		
0:00–0:04	Opener		
0:04–0:08	Agenda/Objectives		
0:08–0:12	Content		
0:12–0:16	Process/Participate		
0:16–0:20	Content		
0:20–0:24	Process/Participate		
0:24–0:28	Content		
0:28–0:32	Revisit		
0:32–0:36	Content		
0:36–0:40	Process/Participate		
0:40–0:44	Content		
0:44–0:48	Process/Participate		
0:48–0:52	Q & A		
0:52–0:56	Revisit		
0:56–1:00	Closer		

Lesson Timing Tool

One of the most asked-for templates I have created is the Workshop Quick Timing Flow. It is used to help with timing. If you are like me, I end up counting minutes over and over to see how many minutes I have left.

Name Of Instructor

Class Title Virtual Training Truly PC

Topic to be Taught
Title: _____
Location: _____
Date: _____

*Set **only** the First Start Time (ex 8:00:00am) * then change time allotted for each item in time column table below (ex for 10 minutes 12:10:00)*

Name Of Instructor

Start	End	Time	Item	Materials Needed
9:00 AM	9:05 AM	0:05	Welcome Trainer and Producer	
9:05 AM	9:10 AM	0:05	10 Differences - Chat how different from Live Training?	Whiteboard/Chat
9:10 AM	9:20 AM	0:10	Agenda/Book Walk/Flip and Flag	
9:20 AM	9:25 AM	0:05	Orientation	
9:25 AM	9:30 AM	0:05	webcam and mic check	
9:30 AM	9:35 AM	0:05	Deck of Cards selection	
9:35 AM	9:50 AM	0:15	Vital Signs - Use or lose	Break out rooms - group share
9:50 AM	10:00 AM	0:10	1 - Use Closers	
10:00 AM	10:10 AM	0:10	Openers	
10:10 AM	10:15 AM	0:05	Revisiters	
10:15 AM	10:25 AM	0:10	Energizers	
10:25 AM	10:30 AM	0:05	CLOSER - Quote your tip	
10:30 AM	10:45 AM	0:15	BREAK	
Total		1:45		

With this tool, you just enter the time in the time column in this excel format, and it automatically changes the timing. For the free download, go to https://www.bobpikegroup.com/workshop-quick-timing-flow.

Virtual Platform Tools

The Virtual Platform Tools job aid helps ensure you are using a wide variety of interactivity. Too often I see only the chat area being used for engagement. If you are going to be teaching and training in the world of webinars, engagement is key and having variety is imperative.

Content	Virtual Platform Tools	
	Application Sharing ☐ Case Studies ☐ Demonstrations ☐ Independent Study ☐ Multi-Media Game Show	☐ Raptivity ☐ Round Robin ☐ Spreadsheet Collaboration
	Breakout Rooms ☐ Case Study Review ☐ Debate ☐ Field Trips ☐ Private Breakout	☐ Problem Solving Report ☐ Scavenger Hunt ☐ Skills Practice ☐ Team Competition
	Chat Room Activity ☐ Brainstorming ☐ Conversation ☐ Discussion Exercises ☐ In the Moment Feedback ☐ Paired Share (*if participants can private chat) ☐ Peer Response Reflection ☐ Q&A	☐ Re-Engagement Technique ☐ Scenario Answers ☐ Timed Chat ☐ Terminology Drag and Match ☐ Video ☐ Window Paning ☐ Word Find
	Polling ☐ Anonymous Feedback Assessment ☐ Class Pace ☐ Energizer Questions ☐ Opener – Community Share	☐ Session Feedback ☐ Testing ☐ TurningPoint Technology
	Web Browser Sharing ☐ Competitor Scoping ☐ Group Activity ☐ Marketing Guides Online ☐ Model Filling In Forms ☐ Model Where to Go for Help	☐ Secret Pages Revealed ☐ Video Viewing ☐ Web Tour of Company Website
	Whiteboard Activity ☐ Annotate ☐ Best/Worst ☐ Capture Session Expectations ☐ Case History Chart Labeling ☐ Collaborative Content Changes ☐ Crossword Puzzles ☐ Find and Fix ☐ Graphic Organizers	☐ Graphical Voting ☐ Pictionary Type Games ☐ Highlight ☐ Jeopardy™ Type Games ☐ Matching Game ☐ Mind Maps ☐ Raptivity ☐ Teachbacks

Technology Task List

The Technology Task List is a job aid I run through to make sure I am ready to use the tools for any webinar and that my tech is up to the job. It is a tool for you as the presenter to self-assess your webinar platform, internet and computer. When walking through this checklist, it is important to remember to be in the location with the same internet you will have when you practice.

Content	The Bob Pike Group's Technology Task List
	Webinar Platform ☐ I can utilize all of the tools within the platform with ease. ☐ I know where all the tools are located and which buttons to use. ☐ I know what the platform looks like as a participant. ☐ I have practiced using all the tools and double checked it will work for the size group I am hosting. ☐ I ensured that the virtual classroom is large enough to host the number of participants I have attending. ☐ I know what search engines work best with the platform. ☐ Day before the webinar: I have tested each tool being used on the computer, headset, webcam I will be using.
	Internet ☐ I have a high-speed connection that is reliable. ☐ I have turned off the wi-fi feature on my computer to ensure it is using the high-speed connection. ☐ I have a hot-spot or wi-fi that is working and can be accessed as a back-up. ☐ I have an alternate place to set-up and present from should I need to use last minute. ☐ Should internet go down I have the phone number of someone on the webinar (moderator) who can tell the group what is happening.
	Computer ☐ I am using a reliable laptop or computer to present and not a smart device. ☐ I have a second computer or laptop that is on and logged in as a participant and can be easily upgraded to presenter if needed. ☐ I have a smart device logged in as a participant to recall features being used. ☐ I have fully charged my devices should power go out. ☐ I have an associate in the office who is also on the webinar should I need to use their computer last minute.

Webinar Activity Ideas

Here is a quick-start checklist of activities you can work into your webinar to make it interactive and engaging. Simply look for the type of engagement you want, then look at the different tools you could use to do the exercise. It includes common activities like text chat and whiteboard. This is not exhaustive as the intent is to be a quick start guide for interactivity.

	Text Chat	E-Mail	Video Streams	Audio Stream	White Board	Bulletin Board	Phone
Case Studies	X	X			X	X	X
Crossword Puzzles	X	X					X
Debates	X	X			X	X	X
Demonstrations	X	X	X	X	X	X	X
Dialogues	X	X	X	X		X	X
Games	X	X	X	X	X	X	X
Graphic Stories		X	X		X		X
Interviews	X	X	X	X		X	X
Learning Teams	X	X			X	X	X
Lecture Activities	X	X	X	X	X		X
Lecture	X	X	X	X	X	X	X
Memorizations	X		X	X	X		X
Object Lessons	X	X	X	X		X	X
Panels	X	X	X	X	X	X	X
Projects	X	X	X	X	X	X	X
Questions/Answers	X	X	X	X		X	X
Quizzes	X	X				X	
Reports		X	X	X	X	X	X
Role Plays	X	X	X	X	X	X	X
Sentence Completions	X	X	X	X		X	X
Simulations	X	X			X		
Skits	X		X	X			X
Slides	X	X	X		X		
Small Groups	X	X			X	X	X
Symposiums	X	X	X	X		X	X
Testimonials	X		X	X			X
Video Streaming			X				
Virtual Field Trips	X	X	X	X	X	X	X
Word Associations	X	X	X	X		X	X

Repeatable Design Process

Not good with templates? Do you just want to make sure your participants are learning the content and behaviors in small enough chunks? The Ensure Varied Engagement template is quick. Take what you have already designed and start filling in the template. Although everything should have a purpose before the content is created, I sometimes find that entering in the content and behaviors first helps with the purpose. This is a snapshot into your webinar and provides a space for your moderator to know what you'd like for them to be doing during that time. I add materials onto this template because we often ship participants a box of materials to be used during the session, and this helps to recall when they will be used.

Time (minutes)	Purpose	Content	Behavior	Activity	Moderator Table	Materials

CHAPTER FOUR
Choosing Technology

When considering a platform, the trainer, and producer should be involved in evaluating software and features. Unfortunately, many companies or IT departments choose the platform before they even know what they need their platform to do for them, and then the organization is forced to make it work for all their learning programs.

There are some key capabilities you should evaluate in software if you are just now looking at what technology to purchase for online learning: how many participants can be online at one time, will audio be integrated into the system (Voice Over Internet Protocol or VOIP) or will a conference call bridge be needed, and will participants only access the technology via computer or does it need to be made available on a mobile device. For the purposes of actual teaching and learning, a mobile device is not the first choice as it doesn't allow for full participation on most webinar platforms. Appendix A provides basic features on a variety of platforms if you are able to choose which one you train on.

For a training webinar, each learner will need their own device and reliable access to the internet. Roughly one in five American adults is a "smartphone-only" internet user—meaning they own a smartphone, but do not have traditional home broadband service. However, when attending training where engagement is key, a computer allows for full participation.

Some bells and whistles of new or robust software won't work if your learners are stuck with outdated hardware or weak Wi-Fi. I have had clients who have had a difficult time logging in because of firewall issues their IT team has put in place. If learners cannot easily access training, they become frustrated before the session begins, which can increase anxiety and reduce the success of the training. Consider sending a test link ahead of time to identify any connectivity challenges.

Microphones
One of the most common mistakes I see when training online is trainers who are not using a headset or external microphone. Intermittent audio or audio that is tinny or poor quality makes the experience less desirable

and, frankly, annoying. Just last week, I watched a recorded webinar, and one of the presenters chose to use the pre-installed computer microphone. I was grateful I could fast forward through that section after the first two minutes because it became too difficult to continue listening to the crackling sound. Even a $20 headset off Amazon produces better sound than your Mac or PC built-in microphone.

Built-in mics often pick up sound from all around, from the clacking that comes from typing to the fan humming nearby. This ambient noise is not heard by the presenter, but everyone tuning in can hear it all.

What type of headset or microphone should you choose? Selecting can be a trial and error process. I choose not to use my earbuds with built-in mic because it also picks up too much ambient noise and requires a bluetooth connection, which can fail. I also present many hours a day, and the buds can begin to hurt.

When selecting a mic, keep in mind that any bluetooth product will be less stable than a headset with mic or mic that is plugged into either a USB or headset jack. I use a gaming headset that works with both my PC and Mac (by HyperX). It is bulky and red and fits my big personality. I have an extra as a backup and have other headsets within arm's reach because, if one goes down, I need to be ready with another.

When you begin your search, decide if you prefer a headset or external mic like the very popular Blue Yeti, Blue Snowball Ice, Samson Meteor or Rode Procasters. Each of these has a different price range and provides a different sound experience.

No matter which microphone you are using, it is important to use it well. Consider testing the microphone prior to the start of the session with your producer. Throughout the session, I encourage the use of private messaging so the producer can check in with you on the sound. Sometimes we back off or move the mic, and then we are too loud or too soft, and sometimes we forget to unmute ourselves!

When testing the sound of your microphone, listen for background noise and ambient noise. This is where having a headset can be valuable as it reduces this automatically. When testing, use your normal voice. I know I get excited at times and can become louder, so I also test my "excited" voice to make sure the volume is acceptable.

Webcams

We are in the age of video overload. I am still a fan of having webcams and being able to see one another virtually. However, I continue to utilize webcams only part of the time and have content, the whiteboard, and activities be the focus for the remainder. When I turn on my webcam, I typically have my whiteboard go blank so learners know where their attention should be focused. I also build in a blank, dark slide into my presentation deck to remind me to turn on my webcam then share a piece of content while also turning the learners' attention on me and what I have to share.

Webcams allow for learners to connect with one another and get to know who is on the other end of the training. Having learners use their webcams in breakout rooms can be a very powerful way for them to get to know one another and connect. From time to time, I will have everyone turn on their webcams to celebrate or do an activity. I will also take pictures or screenshots when we're all on together and send out a "class photo." The invention of the "selfie" has helped us get used to looking directly into the camera. Make sure you transfer this skill to your webinar camera, too.

Your computer's internal webcam is typically enough. In my case, I utilize two computers, both of which have built-in webcams, and an additional webcam that is set up in a different part of the room where I may stand and present. There's nothing more awkward than trying to turn your laptop around to try to get a good angle while you're standing and presenting. Believe me, I have done this many times, and it is always awkward. If you present often and you plan to stand and present for a portion of the time, I recommend getting an external webcam.

Lighting

I am embarrassed to share that for the first 15 years I was doing virtual training, I only used the natural light from the windows along with the terrible overhead lighting in my office. Having now done thousands of webinars, I have learned the importance of good lighting.

I would encourage everyone to purchase a ring light and have that directly behind and above your webcam. The one I own is 10 inches and has different tones such as cool blue or warm white. I typically go for the warm yellow because I feel it looks best with my skin tone. I recommend the UBeesize light.

The great thing about using some form of additional lighting is the ability to easily and affordably change the amount of light in the space you are presenting. Lights can be as affordable as $25. I upgraded a bit, and mine came with a wireless remote. This has proven to be worth every penny because I am not busy fumbling with settings on the light itself. I can quickly adjust and then turn on the webcam.

If you do have natural lighting in the room, the windows should be facing you and not be behind you.

Most platforms allow you to see yourself before going live. This gives you a chance to see what lighting looks best and an opportunity to adjust the brightness.

CHAPTER FIVE
Training Platform Tool Overview

If I were to poke my head under the hood of my minivan with monkey wrench and crowbar in hand, I'm sure my spouse would want some reassurance I knew what I was doing. While the physical consequences might not be as dire online, you can cause a lot of collateral damage and create more work by not being familiar with the tools of your webinar platform. Here is a quick tutorial to get you started.

Application Sharing

Application sharing has also been called remote desktop sharing and is a tool that is in almost every platform, whether for trainings or meetings. It functions as a way for people to view each other's desktop applications and collaborate on projects. Some platforms allow for all users to be able to host and share while others only allow for the moderator or facilitator to host. Application-sharing is a great way to make learning meaningful because participants can immediately apply the content.

This tool is most commonly used to demonstrate software or navigate a website before the learner takes control and mirrors the process. This is good if you are hosting a webinar one-on-one or one-on-few because, in a large group, very few participants will get to "drive."

Application sharing can be a powerful tool if a little creativity is used. I really like playing games. Products like AllPlay Web and BRAVO! are two that allow learners to have a virtual response pad, and then the instructor application shares the actual game show and questions. This is a more advanced skill but a fun way to revisit content.

If you are drafting templates, application-share the templates with the learner and together make annotations and modify the documents in real time. When sharing applications, it is critical to have a second computer logged in as a learner so that you are able to walk them around the screen and tell them where to look for information. Keep in mind that there are bandwidth differences and the amount of time it takes for one learner's page to refresh and redraw the screen could be up to a minute different from others.

Although I recommend using the synchronized web browsing to show items on the web, some platforms do not have this option, which means application-sharing is the alternative. If you are application sharing, a word of caution: be sure to close any private messages or confidential documents and take the time to clear out cookies if application-sharing the internet. Five years ago, I was on a sales webinar, and the facilitator shared his desktop to show us improvements to a website. When he began typing the address into his web browser, a drop-down menu appeared showing several other website options that were clearly not for our eyes. I don't think he even realized what we were viewing as he just continued on. I have no idea what the rest of the call was about because I was too busy laughing with the rest of the group.

Below are some questions to consider about your platform's application-sharing function before selecting activities to use from this book:

- Can you application-share a learner's desktop?
- Is the application sharing view only for learners or can they interact with your desktop? What permissions are needed?
- How many learners can interact when an application is being shared?
- Can multiple applications be shared at one time? The entire desktop?
- What are the bandwidth requirements? How do I check to see if my learners are having trouble or how long the lag time is?
- Am I able to change control in the middle of application sharing?

Breakout Rooms

I love using breakout rooms so smaller groups can work together and participate in a more intimate manner. Breakout rooms require everyone to either be engaged or feel like they are letting their group members down.

Breakout rooms, for the most part, are a more advanced tool. I didn't begin using this function until I felt I had mastered other tools because breakout rooms incorporate several of the other tools: whiteboard, text chat, and audio. Those things alone triple the challenge for the end user.

Breakout rooms are great for brainstorming, working on project work, developing concepts, promoting a sense of team through relay races and competitions, or splitting out of a larger group to connect with your smaller territory, pyramid, or job function. When participants have an application time built into the class, which I highly recommend, a personal breakout room allows each learner to post ideas on a personal whiteboard to later report back insights and ideas. I have also used these to connect with my producer while learners are on a break so we can plan the next segment without the whole class listening in.

I have learned it is best to announce that we'll be moving into breakout rooms a few moments before actually doing so to allow the producer time to be ready so she can quickly move learners into the rooms. You may want to have a slide in each breakout room with instructions on what they are to do, even if you've already verbalized the instructions.

For learners that do not have audio capabilities, I encourage them to sign in with their name and after it put "the silent." So it shows up "Dan the silent" so others and I know Dan's responses will be text chatted. This tip comes from hearing myself say too many times, "Joe, go ahead and turn on your mic and share XYZ," and wait only to have Joe text chat, "I don't have a microphone, remember?" When so many people are in a session, it is difficult to keep track of who has audio capabilities, and it makes breakout room work a lot easier when others know the situation. They expect to read Joe's responses.

Below are some questions to consider about your platform's breakout room function before selecting activities to use from this book:

- How many participants can be in a breakout room?
- How many breakout rooms are available for use? Is it limited?
- Can breakout rooms be created prior to participants logging in?
- Can learners be pre-assigned to a breakout room?
- Can slides be pre-posted in each of the breakout rooms?
- When in a breakout room, can participants text chat?
- Can whiteboards from the breakout room be posted in the main room or do they need to be application shared?
- When the session is being recorded, will breakout rooms be recorded as well or only the main room?
- Can a participant be moved from one breakout room to another?
- How do participants let the trainer know they have a question when in a breakout room?

- Will participants be able to hear each other once they are in their breakout rooms if you're using a conference bridge?
- Can music or videos be played in breakout rooms?

Polling

Polling is one of the easiest tools to use, and it is available in every platform to varying degrees. Some platforms have a lot of emoticons users can use while others are very simple and have only hand-raising and pacing features. Polling can be interspersed and done quickly so it becomes a very attractive engagement tool, but it also is one of the most overused tools.

Polling can be used in soft openers and openers as the class begins. It is also a way to receive immediate feedback on session material. At the end of the session, it can be used for evaluations and can be either anonymous or public. More information on designing polling questions can be found in chapter 7.

Below are some questions to consider about your platform's polling function before selecting activities to use from this book:

- What polling options are available?
- Can the results be anonymous?
- Can polls be posted to the whiteboard?
- Is there a limit to the number of polls that can be done?
- Can questions be pre-designed or posted in the moment?
- Which polling options can export a report and be saved?
- Can you export individual learner survey results for testing purposes?

Text Chat

The text chat feature is just what you might guess it to be: a small box in the corner in which participants, producers, or facilitators can type. When the "enter" key is hit, the statement, question, or comment shows up in the public feed for all to see.

I personally prefer to always have the "chat room" open and allow learners to interact throughout the session. It is an easy way for learners to stay engaged, even on their own, and encourages a sense of community. From time to time, the comments may be about something else, but at least you know they are actively participating in the session and still online. The only time I would recommend limiting the text chat feature is if participants are abusing the tool and being inappropriate with their comments.

When learners are asked to text chat their thoughts, be sure to read the thoughts aloud when working with smaller class sizes or purposefully give them time to review their classmates' responses if it is a larger class. This affirms their thoughts and also makes their efforts seem worthwhile. If neither of these two things happens, learners stop participating because they feel like no one cares and that the activity is pointless.

Below are some questions to consider about your platform's text chat function before selecting activities to use from this book:

- Is private text chat available for learners to privately work in pairs?
- If private text chat is available, can the producer and trainer view those messages?
- Can hyperlinks be pasted into the chat area and still be live?
- Can participants copy and paste from the text chat area onto the whiteboard and vice-versa?
- Is text chat limited to a certain number of people at a time or is group text chat available?
- Can access to text chatting be limited by participant?
- Can participants view main room text chats in their breakout rooms?
- If a learner logs in late, will she be able to view a history of text chats?
- Can the text chat history and log be saved and viewed later?
- Is there a limit to the length of characters in the text chat area?

Two-Way Audio

When doing webinars, think about all the ways you can use audio so that you are not the only one talking and straining your voice. For me, the biggest difference between a live classroom and an online classroom was how much talking I did online. Although learners were engaging, I found myself doing more of the announcing of text chats or thoughts on the whiteboard. Having a lot of water nearby helps from drying out and cracking, but hearing my own voice for hours got a bit monotonous for me and the learners.

Listening to a new voice is one way to re-engage a learner, and it is easy to do. Try bringing in learners and letting them share their ideas out loud. They are able to expound on their idea, and it builds a connection to that person. A participant vocalizing how content will be applied also increases his retention of the information.

Keep in mind that two-way VoIP audio can also have lag time for learners, and it is always a good idea to have a back-up plan for the session. Talking too fast or too slow can make learners wonder if there is something wrong. Do your best to use pauses for impact, not for finding your place. Pretend you are a talk-show host. Show enthusiasm and excitement as well as passion through your voice. Do what you would do in the classroom: call on learners, use team leaders to share back with the group, speak at a comfortable pace and use word pictures to describe content. Keep in mind that there is regularly a bit of lag time between you speaking and listeners hearing, so wait for learners to respond before talking again.

To reduce feedback, have learners push their on-off microphone icon. Only the person sharing should have their microphone on. If a learner wants to comment, teach them to raise their hand so they can be called on to avoid talking over one another. Unlike conference calls, multiple talkers cannot be heard at the same time with VoIP.

Below are some questions to consider about your platform's audio function before selecting activities to use from this book:

- Can all learners turn on their microphones and have permissions?
- Does my platform allow for both VoIP and a conference call to be used simultaneously if learners are having streaming problems?
- If learners are on a conference call connected to the platform, can they share when they are in breakout rooms?
- If a learner doesn't have a headset, can they still talk without feedback coming through?

Video

Because of the large file sizes, the video tool is one of the most challenging for most platforms; however, a few platforms have found ways to stream video quicker and better, and it is amazing how far this feature has come.

Most platforms only support webcam streaming and not actual video-sharing because of bandwidth issues. If that is the case for your platform, think about housing a video on your website and sharing the link so that learners can view at their own streaming pace. Try to reduce the file size so slower computer systems can more quickly access and play the file.

If you have a platform that does stream video, practice and prepare timing and gauge how it will work for learners if they have VoIP versus a conference call line. If the conference call is not connected to the webinar platform, the sound may not work.

Below are some questions to consider about your platform's video function before selecting activities to use from this book:

- Does my platform support video feed?
- What are the requirements for users to view the video?
- What codec or player plug-in is needed?
- What resolution is the best for streaming a webcam on my platform?
- Can still pictures from a webcam be taken and shown on the screen so the webcam can be turned off and the image discussed?
- How many webcams can be viewed at a time and what are the bandwidth requirements surrounding multiple webcams being on?

Web Browsing and Tours

Take your class on a field trip into the world wide web using this tool! If planning is done in advance, a trainer can take learners to a web page and have them search for the missing answers in their handouts; with the click of a button, everyone is there. Pretty cool stuff!

Those in sales and marketing have used this tool to its fullest; so much learning can happen by viewing websites and examples for discussion.

If you want to use an interactive word search and have participants do it on their own, this is the tool to use. Any open format content (like HTML5) internet-hosted game can be launched in this manner for learners. Keep in mind that web addresses can work and then break. Make sure they are working the day of the session, and take into account the sites that are being visited. If a site requires a password or is blocked by an organization, the tour may come to an abrupt halt. Prevent this by having various users test the link and see if they are able to access it from their work computer.

Below are some questions to consider about your platform's web browsing and tours function before selecting activities to use from this book:

- What plug-ins and codecs are needed for learners to view content?
- What happens once I get to the website? Do learners have control of their desktops, or can I direct them to follow me?
- Can learners have control of the web tour and select the sites?
- Can learners navigate away from the browsing tour?
- Can each learner use their default browser or do they all have to use the same browser?
- Can hyperlinks and bookmarks be created in advance and used?
- If on a site that is firewalled for some learners, what happens? Is there a workaround?
- What permissions do learners need to have prior to the class?
- Are there bandwidth issues to consider?

Whiteboard

The whiteboard, a multifaceted tool, is the most commonly used tool for a trainer or facilitator because it "houses" the slides that were created. It acts as both the projector as well as your flip chart in the online classroom. If you would normally create a flip chart in the moment, the same would be done in the session, as long as you are able to talk and write at the same time.

Use the whiteboard for directions, collaboration, visual support and engagement. When creating slides, think about which ones are for support and which ones learners will be writing or drawing on. For learners with little webinar experience, it is easiest to only have to find the text tool and write, and not worry about changing font size or color.

The whiteboard allows for creativity and imagination. It is fun to watch learners get creative in how they use their tools to post their thoughts.

On the next page are some questions to consider about your platform's whiteboard function before selecting activities to use from this book:

- How many participants can annotate on the whiteboard at a time?
- Can you upload slides prior to the session?
- Can all documents be uploaded to the whiteboard or just slide decks?
- What tools can be used? (e.g. highlighter, text, drawing, insert images, lines and shapes, and pointer tools)
- Can you see all uploaded slides and jump ahead or go back when needed without clicking through all the slides?
- Does the slide import as a JPEG or does it maintain its HTML5 or animated components?
- Can words and images be moved around on the slide?
- Can whiteboard slides created by the group be saved and exported for further discussion?
- Can breakout room whiteboard slides be moved over to the main room?
- Can permission for tools be turned on and off during the session?
- Can drawings and graphics be erased or removed?
- Do whiteboards maintain their annotations even after moving on to another slide?

CHAPTER SIX
PowerPoint Slide Design for Webinars

PowerPoint is the most used business communication tool next to email. Executives say it is also one of the most poorly used tools and, when in meetings, prefer an old-fashioned presentation that doesn't require PowerPoint. However, when teaching online, this tool is the basis for engagement and replaces both classroom PowerPoint and flip charts.

Good slide decks display content in a clear and simple way while conveying a message quickly. Think of a slide like a billboard. You have three seconds for someone to make sense and meaning out of it. For corporate presentations with lots of graphs and charts, try to limit each slide online to just one graph or chart. You really can't get away with mediocre slides online.

In *Presentation Zen*, Garr Reynolds, a self-termed "design evangelist" and management professor, says people can't listen and read at the same time and, unless you are reading the slide verbatim, your learners are only focusing on listening or reading—not both. If the words match the message exactly, then why not just send the slides and forget the training? Instead, the slide should be an image or picture that represents the message being shared. Whiteboard slides (often created in PowerPoint and uploaded as a presentation) should be interactive and allow for discussion.

Before going further, open up a deck you plan to use or have used in a webinar. Now look at just one slide a few minutes into your presentation. As you look carefully, are there extra words you could remove and still keep the meaning? Extra animation? Too many graphics or the wrong graphic? More is not better. Sometimes it is just more and creates white noise which takes away from the learning and understanding of the slide.

Each webinar platform allows for slides to be uploaded; however, some maintain the animation while others convert the slide into a still image. It's important to know in what way the information is taken into the platform before designing begins. How frustrating to take time creating awesome animations only to discover that they don't work during the webinar!

Webinars with WOW Factor

In the following pages, you will look at just a few PowerPoint design tips. It will not make you an amazing graphic designer but will get you moving down the right path. And a word of experience here: each time you design a slide deck, start with a clean presentation and keep track of which version is the most updated so you don't grab and use the wrong one. Boy, have I done that more than once!

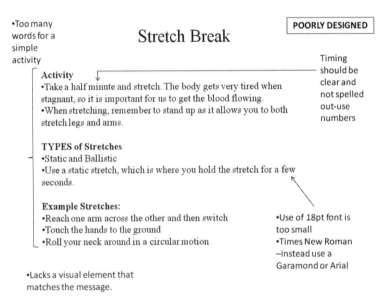

PowerPoint Design Principles

There are many books out there on PowerPoint design, and for every concept I will share, I am sure there are others who will come to a different conclusion. Keep in mind that designing slides for a classroom with ambient lighting or an auditorium with 3,000 people is not the same as PowerPoint with the sole purpose of being on a personal computer or laptop. When creating your slides for a webinar, the following tips can help your slides be more engaging and actually reduce the onset of headaches, which are common when staring at a computer screen for extended periods of time.

Build in White Slides

When crafting your PowerPoint deck for synchronous training, insert slides in advance when you know there will be an exercise where the facilitator, producer, and participants will be asked to write, draw, or do a collaborative exercise. Although inserting a whiteboard on the fly is fairly simple, it is one less step to think about, and it helps to remind the facilitator that an interactivity is supposed to happen.

Utilize Dark Slides with Light Writing

When participating in a webinar, notice the number of slides that are white background with dark words. On the flipside, using slides that are dark with light writing provides a distinct difference from the rest of the platform, which makes it easier for participants to differentiate the whiteboard area from the tools and other application areas of the platform. Why does the contrast matter?

Computer screens use pixels. Each pixel is a point of light on the computer screen that is very bright in the center and fades to nothing on the edges. If an optical muscle is repeatedly flexed over a long period of time, it can lead to a mix of eye and vision problems called Computer Vision Syndrome. It is also commonly believed that fatigued eye muscles lead to headaches, which can cause tension and then tight muscles in the neck, shoulder, and back. One way I reduce the eye tension learners might experience is to limit the amount of bright light on the webinar platform and increase the amount of contrast and definition in images. Another way is to use bolded text and fewer words.

In general, I use slides with a white background for exercises when learners are unfamiliar with the writing tools and changing the color might just be too much for them. These sessions are typically 90 minutes or less.

A light background on slides makes it easier for participant interaction with the drawing tools like the use of color. When you're designing a slide, don't be tempted to choose just any background color because the choice is there; a bright background color or 50 colors doesn't necessarily make a slide more "visual." I recently had a client who used cotton candy pink as the PowerPoint deck background. In general, pink is not a color that should be used for a background. It should be used for things like ice cream and—you guessed it—cotton candy.

Background colors that are appropriate are blues, greens, blacks, deep purple (almost black), deep reds, and grays. The text color should contrast sharply with the dark background. Typically that would include white, yellow, tan, and most bright colors. Colors appropriate for highlighting are orange, yellow and most pastels.

Reduce Words
Use fewer words on your slides, but keep the meaning. Additional text can and should be in the handouts. This is not giving permission to have a thesis for a handout, but merely explaining that slides should have limited words pre-designed.

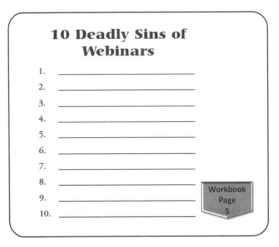

A clean and simple slide before learner participation

For example, I use pre-designed slides that have few words and then learners brainstorm their answers on the whiteboard. By the time we are done, there are a lot of words listed on the whiteboard; this is completely acceptable because the learners are participating and adding the extra content. The whiteboard they saw before the activity began was clean and simple.

When you are done designing your slide deck, run through your presentation for the flow and make changes. On each slide, ask yourself if there is just one message and if that message is Nice to Know or Need to Know.

Reduce Bullets

In 2003, Pulitzer-prize winning columnist Julia Keller wrote an article entitled "Killing Me Microsoftly with PowerPoint." This would be an apt description of many webinars. The overuse of the program's many capabilities cloaks the actual content and inhibits communication. Line after line of text and slides riddled with bullet points and multiple fonts do not create retention. Nor does a plethora of continuous animation, 3-D charts and graphs that, frankly, would be easier to review if they were simple and one-dimensional.

Just because a tool has cool widgets and gadgets doesn't mean you have to use them all. Keep it simple and clean. When using animation, keep it discreet and consistent. This means if you have titles "fly in" from the right, be consistent and use the "fly in" animation for the rest of that slide. It isn't more creative to "fly in" for the first thought and then "box in" for the next.

Cut down the number of bullets you use by limiting yourself to one theme or idea per slide. Having one idea on each slide reduces confusion on the topic being covered, keeps the focus on a single topic and what you are saying, and keeps learners from jumping ahead.

Use Visual Lists

When you do decide a list of ideas will be an effective way of getting your message across, don't just create bulleted points. Try making the list more visual. For example, when creating an agenda for your learners, show your training itinerary as a road map with content signs along the side of the learning superhighway.

Here are two other examples of visual lists:

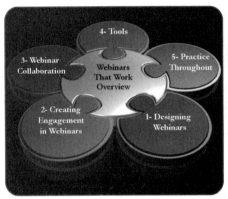 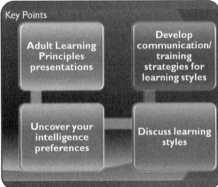

Choose Appropriate Fonts

When we were selling our house, we repainted our daughter's razzle-dazzle rose room a sedate taupe so the color wouldn't overshadow the many features of the home. Just as home sellers try to remove distractions, so should webinar slide designers. Use these three text guidelines when creating your slides:

- Use the 2x2 rule: keep to two fonts per slide and two sizes of font per slide. The title or subject line might be in a size 36 font while the body text might be size 32.
- GET RID OF ALL CAPS. This is not only annoying and considered "yelling" in the world of social media, but it is also difficult to read. All caps should be saved for acronyms, word puzzles, acrostics, and other special purposes.
- Depending on the topic, different fonts might be appropriate for a slide or two. If having learners do an activity of unscrambling words, a SCRABBLE™ font would be creative and clever for that one slide but not appropriate for all slides within the session. Fonts that are easily readable in PowerPoint include sans serif fonts like Arial or Garamond. Fonts to avoid are Times New Roman and scripted fonts. These fonts are more difficult for readers to view online because the letters are closer together. Also, the contrast isn't as crisp, which can increase eyestrain.

Insert Page Numbers on Slides

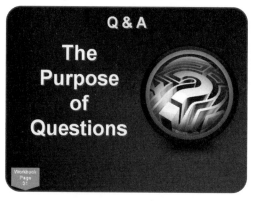

When you are drafting your slides, simply add a subtle page number that corresponds with the page number in the handout. This will help learners who take an unscheduled break find where you are at and jump back into the learning without needing to ask another learner or the producer.

Be Consistent with Title Slides

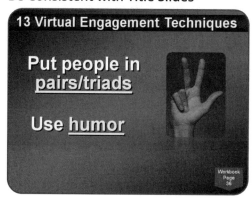

Title slides should have the same title as what is in the workbook or handout. It is frustrating to listen to an instructor talk about a slide titled Change Management when the workbook page is labeled Managing Change in Corporate America. If you want to limit words, like a long title on the slides, make sure you use the same, shorter title in the handbook. Each graph should also have an identifying title or name so that learners know what it is about or where to locate it in the future.

Add Value Beyond the Slide

When teaching a synchronous class, only share need-to-know content and use slides to complement that information. The handout has the need-to-know information, and the slides create a picture of what is being shared to more fully engage the learner by using another of the five senses. Slides should tell a story and allow the imagination to fill in the blanks.

Use Graphics that Enhance the Message

When you use images, they need to take your content to the next level. If you are teaching about customer service, don't insert an irrelevant image of a character running because it's cute. Instead use a picture of you and your friends at Disney World. Why? Because Disney is known for its high level of commitment to great customer service. The image can now move your learners into a text chat about what comes to mind when you think of Disney World and customer service, and from there to messages your company wants to communicate about customer service.

Slides Should Have a Concept

No matter how you design it, each slide should fit the context. The SCRABBLE word scramble is an example of this. That font creates an image in our minds. Even if a learner has never heard of SCRABBLE, the concept doesn't take away from the learning; it only enhances it for those who have had experience with the game. It provides a link to something they already know, which is a way to help people file information and increase retention. The more links one can make to prior knowledge and memories, the more memorable the learning.

Create Pre-Made Question Slides

When you ask participants to interact by answering a question in some way, it is easier for them to do so if they can both hear and see the question. Often people get into their assigned breakout rooms and the first question they ask is, "What are we supposed to do?" They then spend the time trying to figure that out and are not brainstorming answers. To help avert this scenario and save precious time, have the question placed in each of the breakout rooms or in the main room to move the exercise along.

How Many Slides

In the classroom, I assume that each slide will take a minimum of one minute, and I won't have more than 60 slides in a one-hour training. Even 60 is too much, but it provides me with a guideline.

When teaching online, there are no tried and true rules because learners interacting with the whiteboard and a single slide may take three minutes or it may not. So what I recommend is time yourself while running through your presentation and slides. Then add in the amount of time you think the interactive slides will take.

If you are including video in your PowerPoint deck, or just as an add-on in the webinar platform, include a Plan B. I have the same video on a backchannel on our website also. That way, if someone has slow bandwidth or is unable to view it, I have another option to use or to send them.

CHAPTER SEVEN
Polling—The Webinar Multi-Tool

Because you can't see your learners during a webinar, you need to utilize other methods of gauging learner energy and motivation. Polling is a great and speedy way for the presenter to "see" what is going on with participants. Many training platforms have a variety of ways to poll your learners so you can mix it up and not have it become stale.

Different platforms have varying levels of polling capability. Some allow for multiple-choice polls and pacing while others may allow for only yes/no, check-mark and X-in-the-box responses. These tools were built into the platform to help monitor where learners are at with the content in regard to speed and understanding but also work nicely for creating quick quizzes to assess learning.

There are several ways to utilize the polling tool all throughout the webinar. Use it at the beginning to pre-test learners' knowledge of the topic or as a soft opener to have learners answer trivia or personal questions to begin community-building. You can also create surveys to determine interest in a topic or as a re-engagement technique merely by having participants indicate their feelings about the pace of a section.

When using this feature, know what polling and survey tools are available in your platform, whether or not you are able to share results immediately or in a delayed fashion, and if feedback is anonymous.

Below are some guidelines for how best to create and use polling for quiz questions, multiple-choice questions, matching items and post-testing.

Creating and Implementing Quiz Questions
- Purposeless quiz questions are not a good use of webinar time. Make sure questions require higher-order cognition and not just merely fact recall. Don't ask "What does the 'C' in CORE stand for?" Instead, ask something like "Which of the following is an example of a closer?" The second question makes the learner look for what principles apply to a closer while the first merely requires recall.

- I would also suggest writing quiz questions section by section. Good quizzes are difficult to write, and the task is best done one at a time.
- Let learners know if guessing on a question is acceptable or if they should select "do not know" as the answer. This is especially key if you are doing a pre-test and want to know exactly where the group is at. For the post-test, determine whether the same rules apply.
- Use a visual timer to show the amount of time for each question or let learners know how long the poll will stay open. Also, let them know if answers can be changed or if it stays selected once it is chosen.

Multiple-Choice Polling
- Express the full problem in the stem, or main statement. Make sure participants can understand the problem before reading the alternative answers. Usually, direct questions are clearer than sentence completions.
- Put all relevant material in the stem. Do not repeat phrases in the options if the phrase can be stated in the stem.
- Keep the stem short. Unnecessary information confuses participants and wastes their time.
- Make the incorrect answers plausible. Incorrect answers should represent errors commonly made by participants. The best wrong answers are either too general or too specific; accurate but do not fully meet the requirements of the problem; or statements that appear correct. Avoid words that are too extreme such as "always," "never," "all," or "none" as few ideas or situations are absolute or universally true. On occasion, I have found that inserting a humorous incorrect answer lets participants laugh, which reduces tension which increases retention.
- Limit the number of optional answers. Robert Frary, in his book *Practical Assessment, Research & Evaluation*, provides a few facts on drafting multiple-choice questions:
    o Having three answer options is about as effective as four choices.
    o A four-response answer format is the most popular.
    o Never give participants more than five alternatives.
    o Never have both "None of the above" and "All of the above" as options for a single question.

- Do use "None of the above" as the final option, especially if the answer requires computation. Its use makes the question harder and more discriminating, because the uncertain student cannot focus on a set of options that must contain the answer.
- Make all choices similar in structure and equal in length. Do not give away the best choice by making it longer or more detailed.
- Avoid trick questions and double negatives. Negative phrasing often confuses and makes items unnecessarily complex. This also makes a question more challenging for English Speakers of Other Languages (ESOL) participants beyond what is necessary.
- Avoid typos and watch your grammar. Oftentimes we spend the most time scrutinizing the right answer and incorrect answers are quickly thrown together. When this happens, we may not be as careful with our grammar or typing in both the stem and the answers.
- Vary the position of the best answer. Research shows faculty tend to locate the best answer in the B or C position. Instead, use a deck of cards to locate correct responses randomly. For example, if you pull a heart, put the correct answer in the first position. Draw a spade? Place the answer in B, and so on.
- Keep the test length manageable. From Joseph Lowman's book *Mastering the Techniques of Teaching*, we know participants can only complete between one and two multiple-choice items per minute. Use that information to calculate how much time you'll need for your polling.

Matching Test Items

- Give clear instructions. Let participants know how items are to be matched, where to write answers, and whether a response may be used more than once.
- Keep the two sets of items homogeneous. For example, Column 1 may list events and Column 2 may list dates; do not combine events, dates, and names in one column.
- Try to order the responses. If you order the items in Column 2 alphabetically, chronologically or conceptually, participants will be able to read the series more quickly and locate answers more rapidly than if there is no order.
- Create more responses than premises. In general, give participants five to 10 alternatives in Column 2. If you include distracters in

Column 2, let participants know that some of the entries in Column 2 do not apply.
- Be conscious of the layout and format. Always keep both columns on the same page so that participants don't have to flip back and forth. Place answer blanks to the left of each entry in Column 1. Place Column 2 on the right-hand side of the page. Use capital letters for the responses (they are easier to discern than lowercase letters) and numbers for the premises.

Post-Test Item Analysis
- Use the results to improve your tests. If everyone in the class is getting a quiz question wrong, think about revising or rewording the question. If the question is too difficult or too easy, think about throwing it out and creating a new one that will be more fair.
- Solicit participants' comments about the test.

CHAPTER EIGHT
Participant Handouts– A Trainer's Secret Weapon

As I was preparing a handout for a conference presentation, I noticed a survey in my email inbox asking whether or not I could do my session at that conference without handouts. After I responded, I received an email from this organization stating they would not be printing handouts in an effort to go green. I got riled up and decided I would print my own.

A handout is a critical tool for engagement and can assist the trainer in meeting the various visual and kinesthetic needs of learners. Just like a good old-fashioned thank you note, well-designed handouts should never go out of style. They are appreciated and re-read by many recipients and, if you've done your design right, a valuable job aid to be used for continued reference.

Handouts also provide a way for learners to work on their own for a short time, which meets the needs of the reflective learner. Being a part of an interactive webinar is great for the active and participative learner, but the reflective learner needs time to absorb, process, and work alone. By designing handouts that allow for independent study, you are recognizing the needs of all types of learners.

People in general are highly visual. That tendency can help bridge the comprehension gap left by an auditory message and bring learners to a conclusion much quicker. In the book *Made to Stick*, Chip and Dan Heath point out that concrete concepts are more memorable than abstract. Handouts can help bring abstract ideas into a more concrete or clear message, thus making it easier to learn and remember.

Handout Principles
- Don't use a copy of your PowerPoint deck as your handout. If your slides are designed well and your webinar is truly participant-centered, it wouldn't do the learner much good anyway. If you do not have time to modify your deck right away, at the very minimum, remove some of the words and replace them with a blank line for learners to fill in.

- Follow the same 2x2 principle as for PowerPoint design. Designers should keep to two fonts and two sizes of font per page. Too many fonts and font sizes distract the participant from the message being shared. Remember to keep it clean.
- Make your handouts interactive. When someone starts a task and gets interrupted, the brain continues to search for completion. When there is a fill-in-the-blank on a page, most people, whether they are note-takers or not, want that blank filled in and will look for the right words in order to fulfill that subconscious need. If a facilitator skips the fill-in, many learners will be quietly annoyed and will try to figure out a word that makes sense. Oftentimes they will raise their virtual hand and ask for the answer to that missing blank.
- Use clear images that match the message and have a clean look and feel. This helps to draw learners into the workbook. When a page is disorganized or cluttered, participants will regularly look away and throw it away after the session.
- Number the pages. In writing this book, I printed off drafts not once but twice without page numbers and had no idea where I was at or what page to direct one of my editors to. It takes a lot more time to find something when there isn't a clear way to get to it. And if handouts aren't numbered, they won't match the slide deck page number. It's a detail easily overlooked, and it's much easier to find a page by number than by title.
- Divide your handout into sections. At the very least, create a "need-to-know" section and an appendix. If you have a large workbook, think about using tabs for easy reference or have learners create and insert their own tabs. One of my first Bibles had a tab for each book. It was much quicker to find one of the 66 books before I memorized them. And, because your learners most likely won't be memorizing where chapters are, tabs make sense.
- Send out handouts in advance of the session. Let learners print off the workbook and be ready for the class to begin. Sending a large file the day of the event can cause many frustrations and headaches, and tempts Murphy's Law.
- The appendices of this book model several good handouts with job aids, charts, grids and reference material to aid in learning. You could also insert in-home study or project work as well as flow charts and marketing collateral. Having the information up close and personal can help when a slide just isn't big enough.

CHAPTER NINE
Secrets of a Powerful Presentation

Bryan Lankin once said, "A presentation cannot make a career, but a presentation can undo a career." Now that you have done the hard work of designing and developing an amazing session, don't ruin it with poor presentation.

If you were to name your top tips for powerful presentations, would they include putting energy into your voice, conveying passion, dressing for the occasion, ending on time, or avoiding filler words? Let's look at a few things you can do to "dress up" the presenting portion of your program.

Be Prepared

Until tenth grade, I had never done an official presentation outside of English class. But sophomore year, I decided to run for student council. Just thinking back to that presentation makes my heart race. I could not have anticipated what was to come.

In front of hundreds of peers at the pep fest, I approached the podium and began presenting when, without warning, three boys in the top left section of the stands began booing me. No one came to my aid. I continued my presentation, humiliated, and made it through. I was mortified, and yet I stayed in school the remainder of the day, head held high. I took the bus home, ran to my room, and cried into my pillow for what seemed like hours.

This formative experience, even decades later, motivates me to be prepared for anything. When I take the stage, face fear, and follow the plan, it works out. Fear can keep people from reaching their full presenting potential.

Passion also makes a difference. I ran for student council, not because I had a passion for it, but because I wanted it on my transcript. Now I speak and present on ideas about which I am passionate with plenty of practice and preparation, and that recipe has made the difference.

Creating a webinar with high impact requires overcoming your fears of failing and preparing to give your best presentation. Even if you don't consider yourself a trainer or speaker in general, it is now expected in most positions that at some point you will be the presenter. Look at it as a way to stand out from the crowd and showcase your knowledge and abilities.

Flow

Start with, at minimum, a high level flow or concept of how the presentation will evolve with bullet points of ideas and concepts. If you don't know a piece of content, write it out or at least the research citations. Practice by recording the session and re-watching it. Keep what went well and ditch the sections that did not. I have a weekly podcast and I sometimes will record one and then rerecord. The second is always shorter and more succinct.

When practicing, keep in mind the sections that you must share and if there are any "Nice to Know" pieces that can be discarded in the moment, highlight those. One never knows when the amount of time we are given may be cut short. Knowing what can be cut in advance makes thinking on your feet much easier.

Take Deep Breaths

Anytime you're starting a brand new session, you may start to get the hand sweats, your heart may be pumping a little faster than usual, and your voice might be shaky.

Deep breathing helps slow the heartbeat which then allows our voice to come across more clear and less nervous. For this exercise, count to six as you deeply inhale through your nose and exhale out your mouth. Do this six times. This should calm you and help get your voice under control.

Imagine the Audience

When online, if you do not have everyone on camera, try to imagine who is in the room. If you have met them before, it is easier. In my case, I have never met most of my learners. If I haven't met them before, starting my session with cameras on can be helpful for the remainder of the session so that I may recall faces and feel like I am talking to a group and not just the computer. Just as I use post-its on my computer for reminders, I sometimes put pictures of people smiling at me on my monitor as well. I pick funny and silly pictures because it brings me joy and makes it easier to "see" my audience.

Use Humor
In this day, I would say humor is a necessity. Even industry perfectionists add in a bit of it here and there. When you're nervous, a bit of humor can break the ice. Even if you're not a humorist, it is always good to have a one-liner to use along the way. I write out a few good lines and put them on a note card to use when I need to break the ice because I am never sure exactly when the need will arise. Notice I say use humor and not jokes. Jokes and sarcasm can ruin an otherwise wonderful presentation in the blink of an eye.

If you have an upcoming event for a special group and are not sure of a one-liner or a pun you could use, call a friend and ask for help. Scan industry newspapers and magazines that relate to the subject you are presenting on or the people to whom you are presenting and see if there is usable material there. For example, if I were presenting to a hair salon chain, I might use the line, "I love watching football when I am at the salon. The coverage is the same, but the highlights are much better!"

Keep to the Time
It's hard to find something that sours your learners' disposition to your training faster than saying you will be done at a certain time and finishing five minutes late. Participants will forgive ending early any day of the week, but they do not like to be held after the session ends. The same is true for the start time. Many of us think that waiting for everyone to be online is polite, but instead it rewards those who are running late. Instead of waiting for everyone to arrive, I recommend starting on time and honoring those who are there and ready to go.

If technology is the issue, having a producer will allow you to start on time and still provide help for those learners struggling to log in. When I notice there is a large group of people running behind, I ask the people who are there to enjoy a five or ten-minute break and grab another cup of coffee. Another option is to start on-time and record the session. As those latecomers arrive, I might mention the session is being recorded for all to enjoy at their own pace for the next week. I do not call out those who are late, I just honor those who are ready to go.

Another way to keep to the time is to write out exactly what you are going to say and present it with a timer or go with the rule of thumb that a 60-minute webinar would be about 30 typed pages long, double spaced. I personally do not type out every single word I plan to say unless it is a keynote. In general, I create bullet points with thoughts and ideas and key messaging. By using bullet points, I am able to present from a life lived versus a lesson plan. When I type it all out, I have a harder time sounding natural and have a tendency to stumble over my words. If you do choose to write out your presentation, be sure to read it aloud a few times, and if there is a point at which you stumble after having read it a few times, change it. Keep your sentences short and sayable!

Use the leader's guide, and keep track of timing as the session goes along. If it is a course for credit, have additional content in the learner's handbook that can be covered versus trying to stretch the content. When the pace is slow, distracters abound.

Jargon
When presenting to a professional audience, it can be easy to slip into jargon. If a learner is confused or has to take too much time trying to decipher the term, the confusion overshadows the actual content you're trying to share. My recommendation is to know the audience and, if they speak the language of acronyms you plan to use, then use them. However, if you are unsure about their familiarity with the terms, define them upon first use and spell it out. For example, I may use the abbreviation "ROI" in my training, but upon first use, I introduce the term by saying something like, "When we look at the return on investment, the ROI, for a training program…."

Be Yourself
When I first started training at The Bob Pike Group I learned from some of the best interactive trainers in the world: Bob Pike, Betsy Allen, Doug McCallum, Rich Meiss, and Dave Arch, to name a few. I sat in on many sessions and watched as they masterfully handled the content and interactions. I watched as participants rose to their feet at the end of these presentations, and I took ample notes so that I could mimic what they had just done. I wanted the energy of Betsy, the calm of Rich, the magic of Dave, the knowledge of Doug, and the stories of my dad, Bob.

When I was ready for my certification and presenting my first class, I had done everything to memorize content and repeat what I had seen. The only problem is that it was not me. I didn't have my own voice. I learned that, especially when keynoting, I cannot replicate someone else's style. It takes far more effort and usually falls flat. For a few years, I continued to imitate these amazing people before I realized I had my own stories and energetic, charismatic style.

As you find your own voice, remember to be clear and simple. I watch TED Talks to see how others are succinct with their presentations. Don't throw in language just to look really smart like "could you elucidate that content so I can fully understand?" In this example, the word elucidate is a bit ironic because it means to explain or make something clear. Why not just say "could you explain that again in a different way?"

When my kids first began attending a classical school, I remember my daughter coming home one day with a worried look. I asked her what was wrong. She shared that other students were using really big words during their weekly presentations, and she felt like she was not smart because she wasn't using big words. I told her that it takes a lot of smarts to be able to paint a picture with your words in a way that is compelling and that all may understand. She has now taken years of Latin and Greek and guess what? She chooses not to use big words and has found her own voice.

I love listening to and reading about American presidents. Among my favorites are Ronald Reagan and Abraham Lincoln. They were truly great orators. Quotable. Some favorite lines from Lincoln are "Whatever you are, be a good one," "Folks are usually about as happy as they make their minds up to be," and "No man has a good enough memory to be a successful liar." And Reagan humorously said, "Before I refuse your questions, let me make an opening statement." They each definitely had their own voice.

What You Say Both Verbally and Nonverbally
When presenting, avoid repetitive language and the "ahs" and "umms." Most of those can be avoided just by slowing the pace of your speech. Practice in front of the mirror and slow down and pause for effect.

You can also mix up the presentation a bit with vocal variation. Think of historical orators like Winston Churchill and the strength behind his voice. Or Martin Luther King, Jr., and the cadence to his words. Or your favorite entertainer today and the energy and personality that radiates through his or her voice.

When you do add in vocal variations and gestures, make sure they work with and not against the message. They need to seem authentic to our personalities. Record your webinar and then re-watch it. Observe what's helpful and what distracts. I once had a boss who used the phrase "in theory" 30 times in a meeting. This is distracting and annoying. I cannot tell you what the meeting was about because I was so busy tallying!

I am probably most known for my dramatic facial expressions. I scrunch my nose, roll my eyes, and laugh at myself. I know this from watching myself and have yet to have anyone complain. You need to do you.

Be Logical

I am, by nature, an evaluative listener. I assess verbal content based on the words that are used and make judgements about what is being said. I listen for logic and then decide if I think the speaker is worth listening to, and typically that occurs within the first few minutes of a presentation.

Other types of listeners include appreciative listeners who like the humorous side of the presentation and empathic listeners who relate to your stories and heart. Comprehensive listeners take notes and pay attention and are the people I go to after the session to figure out what I missed.

Just because there are different types of listeners does not mean you have to come up with messaging for each one. Instead, ensure your content flows logically and share from your experience. This, in addition to adding humor, will cover all your bases. Participants have written on evaluations that they liked my sense of humor but have blasted me when my content was not in a logical order or contained too many "kiddish" examples or games. Pragmatic and logical doesn't mean boring!

Question and Answer Time

To garner more questions during Q&A:

- Insert this time two-thirds of the way through your webinar. At the end of a webinar, people just want to log off.
- Turn on your webcam as you ask and answer.
- Think before answering. Even if you have heard the question a million times before, a slight pause for consideration makes it seem as though it were the first time, and for that person it IS the first time. A pause allows for the answer to come across as sincere.
- Pose the question back to the group. There are typically hundreds of years of experience on a webinar, and you can tap into that. I thank the person for the question and then ask the group to take 30 seconds to whiteboard their answers. After sharing some of their ideas, I typically add a few of my own. Adding value beyond their thoughts shows your experience, and no one feels short-changed.
- Don't tout your experience or refer to your accomplishments. Just answer the question directly. An attempt to convince someone of your credibility is usually perceived as the opposite.

Flexibility

A presentation, no matter how eloquent, is a failure if the objectives are not met. You may have spent tens of hours preparing slides and content, but if someone in the virtual room stops your presentation and asks where this is going, the answer is not clicking through more slides. Be flexible, go off course, and tackle the question so you can then get back on track.

If, however, you are missing the mark, do change course. If you feel this is what's happening, find a window of time to ask yourself what the goal of the presentation is to decide best how to continue. I have often had too much content and had to skip slides to ensure we got to the main thrust of what was needed. Be comfortable with being flexible. Put your objectives in front of you. If you start to realize time is running short, know just what needs to be said and skip the rest. Be ready to take 20 minutes of content and boil your position, strategy, or content down to a few sentences. If you are unable to do this, then your objectives are too broad and not as compelling.

Getting and Keeping Attention

When doing a virtual presentation, your participants have the added distraction of technology and websites to surf. Engagement is key from the moment you begin in order to gain participants' attention, and then you need engagement to keep their attention.

Having learners log in and walk away is a disaster. Learning has not occurred, not because you were not well-prepared, but because the participant has so many options and low accountability. This is perhaps why videoconferencing has become all the rage: to ensure everyone is online and not off doing something else. But are they really with you? Don't jump to conclusions if someone appears to be browsing the internet. They may be researching your topic or looking for something related to your message. Plan in exercises that grab attention and ask for opinion.

I once had an awful audience. Some were checked out, but that was the least of my worries. The bigger threat to the presentation succeeding was the online chat that criticized the concepts and my delivery. Sometimes you alone are unable to rally the troops. In this case, I made it through day one and then shared with their managers what occurred. Together we modified objectives, and I enlisted their help for the next day.

When we started the session, the managers shared how relevant this information was and how they looked forward to their next status meeting with each employee to hear how they were applying the new concepts back on the job. My pride took a hit when I couldn't get them back on track on my own, but being humble and asking for assistance helped day two and three become successes.

One simple way to engage and reengage your audience is to use the camera intermittently. There is no need to have it on the entire time unless it is a meeting and you are the main speaker or you are doing a keynote. Remember, the human brain can only focus on one thing at a time, and if you have your camera on while also asking learners to look at a slide, the brain has to choose what to focus on. Unless you are saying the exact words that are on a slide, their brains are either reading the slide or listening to you. And, when you have the camera off then turn it on, it gives learners something new to look and focus on, which in turn reengages them.

Reading Your Online Audience

One helpful task of a producer is tracking participant attendance and progress. When put into breakout rooms, producers are able to join and "see" who is engaged and still in the workshop. If it is important for all attendees to listen to a portion of a presentation so that they may make a decision, you will need to have their webcams on so that you can "read" the room. In training sessions, reading the room is watching nonverbal clues. Instead of asking for their attention or shushing them, which comes across poorly online, read the room and choose a good time to turn off the text chat or regain their attention with a quick poll. If there are particularly challenging individuals, perhaps ask them specific questions like, "Becky, are we on the right track with this conversation?"

With the webcams on, you can also see if a decision maker or someone vital to the outcome leaves the room. If this happens, don't be afraid to ask if the virtual session should be rescheduled or if the decision can be made without that person.

No Eating or Chewing

Trying to talk with something in your mouth, like a piece of gum or a bite of your lunch, makes for a very jumbled presentation. When teaching online, it may not seem like a big deal when the camera is off, and they can't see you. However, the obstruction in your mouth makes your speech more difficult to understand and can cause other problems as well. One particular day, when I had been doing back-to-back webinars, I hadn't had time to eat. So I decided to snack on the pecans in my drawer while participants were working on an assignment. Bad move. My mouth became very dry, and the next segment was spent muting myself to drink water. I would have been better off with a growling stomach.

What about drinking? If the webcam is off, you can easily take a quick sip of something. I recommend room temperature water over cold for the simple reason that colder fluids move through your body at a faster rate, so you may end up needing a bathroom break sooner. If you are on camera and really need a sip of water, make sure your water is in a clear glass so everyone can see exactly what you are drinking.

Reduce Technology Issues

Ugh. The dreaded technology, unfortunately the most important piece of a webinar. Because you will have participants who have not used the platform you are using, it's important to start with clear directions on how to interact and engage during the session. I put screen shots of the platform on slides and walk learners through, while practicing, what tools will be used.

When I first send out the invitations to the class, I also include links for them to ensure they are able to login to the program and have the technical requirements needed to do so. I find that sometimes when my contact will test it out, they will have firewall issues or cannot connect through their VPN and need additional help. Having this done prior to the event helps prevent issues the day of the session.

Part of the pre-workshop email also includes information on whom they can contact the day of the session should they have technical problems, and the name and email address of my producer. We also send materials in advance of the session to avoid technical issues they may have trying to download materials. If, however, learners misplace those hard-copy handouts, we do have them available to download and design each handout as a fillable PDF.

Reduce Noise

First, don't wear jewelry that may bring added noise. This is noise that I am responsible for and can easily manage. And put your tech notifications on silent. I can manage the ding on the computer when a new email comes in or the alert on my phone that notifies me that I have a text message. I can also control the clacking of my nails on my keyboard, shuffling of papers, coughing and slurping my drink.

Noise that is a bit harder to control is that caused by those around you. I was recently presenting a webinar while our neighbors were having their concrete driveway redone. The jackhammers were so loud! Thank goodness I was wearing a noise cancelling headset with a microphone that is close to my mouth. Yes, it was distracting for me, but at least my learners were not also distracted.

Because there are times when I and my four kids are working and learning from home, I do my best to communicate with them whether they can come in my office or not. A red piece of paper on the door tells them not to enter unless they are bleeding. A yellow piece of paper means you can enter only if really necessary and to find Dad first. And, of course, green paper means they can come on in.

Sometimes, though, having a coworker or kid come in can be an in-the-moment re-engagement technique. Despite my red, yellow, and green paper system, my youngest son, Lucas, seems quite color and paper blind and walks right in and over to my desk.

I have tried giving him "the look" to leave, but he seems oblivious to my nonverbal communication. Now when he comes into my office during a webinar, I have him say hello to the audience on camera quickly, I answer his question, and then I have him say goodbye. I think the audience feels a bit more connected to me because it is real life and if they were with me they would have been a part of it. Obviously, I take into consideration who is on the webinar, and if it is unacceptable, I get people texting in the chat area, turn off my webcam, mute my mic, and then answer his question quickly. I have found this to work far better than trying to ignore him. He's like a bad habit and just keeps coming back!

Noise caused by participants can also be managed. At the beginning of a webinar, I teach learners how to turn their microphones on and off on the platform. We also use the raise hand tool when someone would like to share so we don't have multiple voices sharing at once. Because we use VOIP for our webinars, multiple people speaking at once can create a horrible reverb so teaching this early on is important. Some platforms also give the host (trainer or producer) the capability to mute any or all participants.

Dealing with Distractions

While you may not be able to control the distractions your audience has in their space, you can become aware of distractions you produce. I have been told that I swivel my chair. In order to reduce this, I have put a pillow behind my back which forces me to sit up straighter, which in turn has reduced the swiveling. I also unconsciously bounce my leg which moves my body slightly, something else I have had to work on. I have noticed other trainers fidget with pens, markers, paper, toys, and the list goes on. In person, it looks bad, and online, it is magnified by the camera being focused on you. If this is you, remove everything you can from your desk so there is no temptation.

Speaking of your desk, keeping it clean is important. Have a place for everything. In my session, I have a place for my leader's guide, workbook, glass of water, clicker for my light, and other materials I will need to model on camera. By having my workstation the same every single time, I am not searching for the things I need. My dad taught me that seeming unprepared is as bad as being unprepared because there is no difference to the audience. An uncluttered workstation also makes it easier to find reference material and the session flows you've worked out.

Know the Content

When I'm facilitating, I don't need to be an expert on the content—I just need to know a little bit more than those I'm teaching. If you are teaching a topic that may have a lot of specialty questions, such as the roll out of a new software or system, invite a subject matter expert (SME) to participate in the webinar as a guest speaker to answer any detailed questions and build question-and-answer times into the webinar. Prepare the SME in advance, and use a timer that all can see to help stick to the timing allotted for the session.

Class Size and Camaraderie

How many people should be in a class? For training purposes, I recommend 25 learners to one producer and one facilitator. Each additional participant makes it more difficult to manage the class, engage all learners, use the tools, and have learners feel connected.

When I was producing for a colleague, he greeted the participants and asked them questions, and they turned on their microphones to respond. I could hear interest by both sides and feel the camaraderie, although I could not see it. The relationships built prior to the session, continued all throughout the session, and learners found themselves not wanting to miss a moment.

When you feel responsible to someone else in the room and are held accountable to everyone through participation in polls, breakout rooms, material reviews, and teach-backs, it is far more difficult to get distracted by all the other things online and in the office. The bigger the class, the more difficult this rapport and accountability is to establish and maintain—though not impossible.

Prepare to Teach in the Online Medium
One of the most common reasons webinars do not go well is because of user error with software. When hosting a webinar, practice the online tools, and be familiar with any tools that will be used. Tools could include those within the webinar platform, those applications that might be shared, and conference-calling technology. Familiarity with these also increases facilitator confidence and reduces anxiety.

Preparing includes practicing everything from logging in and uploading the slides to walking through each slide and tool to be used. For example, if an application is going to be shared from one desktop to another, it is imperative the facilitator and producer know how to manage the tools to do this seamlessly. It also helps the producer and facilitator understand how their roles will work together.

Co-Facilitating Transitions
If you are co-facilitating, then do a walk-through of how transitions will happen. When first co-facilitating an online session, novices will often say exactly what is going to happen: "I am now going to hand off the session to Steve who will talk about the next slide." Instead, work together to have easy transitions between facilitators. Do this by having one facilitator setup and lead an activity and the other debrief the activity that feeds into the next content piece. See Appendix L *Checklist for Co-Facilitation.*

Experience It as a Learner
It is important to not only be able to technically share the application but also experience the application sharing as a learner. In some platforms, when application sharing, the learner's desktop doesn't show the whole application unless the user enlarges the window with the application. Unless the facilitator has experienced the tool as a learner, this little fact may get passed by, and participants may get lost in the sharing and not say anything. When these little things are discovered, keep a log of what to say to participants so they can be successful.

Have a Backup Plan
What will you do when the system fails or the conference bridge goes out? When working with technology, it is very common that something

will happen during a synchronous training. Having a backup plan allows for flexibility and usually pays off.

If the platform boots learners off, having a plan as simple as saying, "Let's take an 'een' break! Time for caffeine, nicotine, latrine, magazine or answering machine. Thirteen-minute break and meet back in the virtual classroom. This gives you enough time to do a couple of things but doesn't give you enough time to do all! You choose. See you in thirteen!" I got this from a participant years ago and have been using it faithfully ever since.

Perform
When it is go time, be dynamic. Co-hosts that are diverse "characters" add interest (men, women; voices that are different; perspectives that are unique). It also provides an opportunity to role model the qualities of collaboration you want to instill in others.

If you have prepared well, your PowerPoint will be a great slideshow used as a visual backdrop. This sets the stage for a great, engaging session. Learners will know right away that you won't be reading to them and will appreciate it.

Keeping your 4-minute timed agenda is helpful, but have it flow naturally. You can use a roadmap for your learners with key content pieces but no timing listed so they know what's ahead.

Break Timing
Make sure that the planned breaks happen between the 60-90-minute time frame. Learners need a chance to rest their tired computer eyes, stretch, and use the restroom. You will thank yourself when both you and the participants come back invigorated and ready to absorb more information.

Celebrate!
Before ending, help everyone see how much they accomplished together by having the learners summarize their top takeaways and key facts. Ending with time for learners to reflect on the content and add key learnings to a notes page allows each participant to find the "what's in it for me" element.

CHAPTER TEN
Stage Presence

Growing up, I was a thespian, and my early stage training helped prepare me for my career in the lights of the webinar. There are a lot of similarities between the theatre and being on camera in a webinar.

However, teaching online is also different because you have the added layer of distance. It is like standing up in a presentation behind a lectern. It is a road block between you and the audience. Here are some ways to break through that fourth wall and invite your audience into your webinar story.

Eye Contact
In an online format, looking directly into the webcam is the equivalent of eye contact. This means you are not looking down at your notes. To practice doing this, consider doing a few Skype or FaceTime calls with a family member or a friend. Ask them to specifically give you feedback on eye contact. Ask them what it looks like when you are reading your notes slightly below the webcam versus when you are looking directly at the camera. Is there a big difference? Small? How does it make them feel?

Facial Expressions
In a webinar, facial expressions do not need to be as large as in person because the camera is right there on you. Enthusiasm is contagious, but so is boredom! If your face says you are bored, you can be sure your audience will follow your lead. Instead, communicate with raised eyebrows and a smile. If the topic is serious in nature, a calm face will be as effective as a furrowed brow. Before you begin your presentation, practice laughing, smiling, and moving your facial muscles in general. Just as singers warm up their vocal chords, you should warm up the most prominent feature on camera: your face.

Tying into this is where to aim your webcam. Ensure that the webcam is at the same height as your face or slightly higher. Having the camera aim up from below makes the face look larger and gives an unappealing view of the presenter's nostrils.

Voice

I dare say that some would think a monotone presentation is more believable than one that seems overly enthusiastic, but in the setting of a webinar, enthusiasm fares far better. When presenting online, the barrier of the computer screen means the presenter has to be the one conveying all the "energy" in the classroom. While participants may be laughing along, their fellow participants cannot see that, and the presenter cannot use that energy.

If you are an extrovert and used to being charged by your learners in a classroom, you may find doing a webinar exhausting, far more tiring than presenting live. While you may be tired, don't let your facial expressions show it because a change in facial expressions also changes your voice. So be sure to always smile as you present.

Another way to vary voice is to have another presenter speak on a topic or have a learner share their ideas. The change in voice can reengage a learner and is a nice change of pace. I have a producer during my sessions. They usually start the webinar 20 minutes early and ensure everyone is logged in. They also go through some soft opening slides, and this is a chance for me to jump in from time to time in a jovial way and warm up the crowd. Because of their facilitation of the soft openers, the participants are familiar with the producer, so if my computer should fail and he or she jumps in to cover for me, the transition is not as disjointed as it would otherwise be.

Gestures

Online hand gestures are hardly seen, unless you are presenting from a distance with the camera capturing your body language. When presenting online, you need to think about how you could use hand gestures to aid in the learning process. For example, in our classes at The Bob Pike Group, we have gestures that represent content. When teaching those concepts, we turn on the camera and teach the hand motion that goes along with it. When we teach the importance of having an opener and the keys to opening, we use hand motions to help learners remember. We turn on the webcam and teach raising the BAR (Break preoccupation, Allow networking and Relevant to the content) with openers. For break preoccupation, we clench our hands into fists and place them next to one another and make a breaking motion, like snapping a twig in half. This represents the concept of breaking preoccupation as participants enter the room so they are no longer focused on the phone call they just received or the dishes needing to be done. Once preoccupation is broken, learners are ready to engage in the learning.

When using your hands to gesture, try to be far enough away from the camera that your hands are able to be away from your chest, otherwise you begin to look like a tyrannosaurus rex. I naturally speak using both hands. If I notice my gestures becoming repetitive, I move to only using one hand.

Makeup and Jewelry

I rarely wear anything other than mascara on a daily basis; however, a dear friend shared with me the importance of makeup when on camera, and it was no longer a choice. She has been on TV many times and cares about how I come across. What is the point of good lighting if I don't look good or if I have a glossy face?

For both men and women, here are some tips to help you appear your best on camera.

To prevent your skin from looking oily, wear a bit of foundation and then put powder over. I use powder that matches my skin tone and keep it nearby for retouching, especially when I have my ring light on for extended periods of time. The light gets quite warm. Research shows that men who choose to shave their heads or are bald are seen as more confident. Keep that confidence but also beware of the shine on camera. Powder works well here, too.

As far as make-up choices, use your favorites. If you're not sure what that is, here is what my friend recommended to me as her top "on camera" choices:

- **Foundation:** Make Up For Ever Ultra HD Invisible Cover Foundation (pump)
- **Under Eye Concealer:** Laura Mercier (in the little pot)
- **Blush:** MAC in mocha
- **Mascara:** L'Oreal Lash Paradise
- **Lip Color:** Pinky-brown semi-permanent

- **Necklace:** Nothing too flashy or large
- **Jewelry:** If wearing a headset, do not wear earrings. If wearing earbuds or using a Yeti-type microphone, try small to medium earrings, but again nothing flashy. I do like to wear a necklace to bring color close to my face.
- **Other Visible Piercings:** It may not matter, but if it is possible that your piercings would take away from the message, consider removing additional cartilage studs, or tongue and orbital piercings, for example.
- **Glasses:** If you can see without them, remove them. The glare from lights and the computer screen is noticeable, even if they are anti-glare.

On Camera Advice
- If you are lighter skinned, avoid a lot of white coloring (like a white shirt) around your face as it will wash you out. If you are darker toned, brighter colors around your face look great and take five years off your age.
- Assume everyone is looking at you.
- Always sit up straight. If slouching is a bad habit, post a note that says, "Sit up straight."
- If you disagree with another presenter, be careful not to show it on your face.
- While listening to participants, think about your expression.
- Boredom is visible!
- When you're sick—mute, mute, mute. The sounds of someone blowing their nose and coughing is awful for both presenter and participants. Turn the camera off more frequently. Take medication before the session starts and NOT on camera. Don't apologize for what your learners may not know. Talking about being sick draws negative attention.
- Look through the camera. Allow others to see your eyes. You are seen as more believable if your gaze is kind, direct, steady, smiling, and honest.
- Keep your hair out of your eyes and face. Whether live or on video, playing with hair is distracting. Remember to keep your hands off the face and head in general. Stock hairspray for those video conference days!

- General grooming:
  - Nails should be clean and trimmed. Every hand gesture on camera can be visible.
  - Check for lint and dandruff before session and at breaks. (Pro tip: keep a lint roller nearby.)
  - Shave right before.
  - Check for hair around nose, ears, and neck and trim.
  - Make sure your clothes are unwrinkled. You might keep a steamer handy.

CHAPTER ELEVEN
Deadly Sins of Webinars

Think about your last frustrating webinar experience. What was the problem? Why wasn't it a 10 on the scale of greatness? Chances are at least one of the deadly sins of webinars was committed. Part of avoiding sins is knowing what they are and what to do if unforeseen challenges come up. There are four people who can commit sins and, as the facilitator, you are the one responsible for preventing them!

Deadly Sins Committed by Facilitators

The facilitator is responsible for the entire learning community: how content is shared, timing and pacing, interactions of the learners, and so on. Here are just a few of the deadly sins that the facilitator is able to control and prevent if she takes the time to do so in the planning stage. This list also describes a lot of the roles and responsibilities of the trainer/facilitator.

Not Starting or Ending on Time

Log in early and reward those ready to go by starting on time. If you regularly start late, learners who are ready will learn there's no point in being punctual. I use the first few minutes to review briefly how to use the tools for the day. If learners miss that, they will be frustrated because they don't know how to participate fully; have the producer watch who isn't in the room and have him work with those people on an individual basis. Let learners know in advance that the first few minutes will lay the groundwork for a successful session. If they can't make it on time, send a playback link to a previously recorded mini-session that goes through how to use the platform tools.

Not Having a Soft Opener

A few slides to begin engaging the learners before the session helps to warm up the brain similar to warming up before a run. Soft openers could be puzzles, word pictures, visual images, or word searches. Skip the scrolling slides that only welcome participants and begin creating a learning community. Use a soft opener to break preoccupation and get participants thinking about the content.

Not Having a Handout

Even if the handout is only an empty page that allows for interaction with the content, it is a start and much better than having no direction for learners. Most people want to know, even at a high level, what is going to be covered and what the key elements are. I have a hard time listening to keynote speeches that do not have a handout. Oftentimes, I am left feeling like we jumped all over, and I'm not sure what I'm supposed to take away. Was there a point? Or was I just supposed to be entertained or motivated?

Handouts create clarity and incorporate at least three principles of how people remember:

- Handouts are visual,
- It is easier to recall information when learners have recorded it, and
- Sections are chunked so it's easier to absorb and assimilate information.

No Backup Plan

Ten people are ready to log in and the link doesn't work; now what? It's always best to plan for the worst and hope for the best. In Appendix M, you will find some possible problems you might encounter using technology and best practice solutions.

Too Much Content

Webinars are for "need-to-know" information only. If learners won't be using the information multiple times in the next 30 days, the chances are slim that it will be retained when it is finally needed. Instead, teach learners how to search for the nice-to-know information and practice that multiple times so when the time comes and the information is needed, they know how to go about finding it. Challenge subject matter experts on what is truly need-to-know information. It takes about 33 percent more time to train online interactively compared to the classroom, which squeezes out the nice-to-know information.

Not Enough Interaction

Plan some interaction every 4 minutes. If I plan a poll and it takes 2 minutes to complete, then I need to have another engagement 4 minutes from the time the poll ends. A schedule might look like this:

Total Time	Timing of Interactions (Every 4 minutes)	Topic/ Content	Type of Interaction	Materials/PPT
7:55-8:00	7:55-8:00	Soft Opener	Word search	Hyperlink
8:00-8:05	8:03	Opener	Map locator	
8:05-8:10	8:07, 8:10	Agenda/ Objectives	Fill-in-the-blanks	Agenda slide
8:10-8:25	8:14-8:18, 8:22	Content	Whiteboard, brainstorming	
8:25-8:35	8:26-8:31, 8:35	Content	Read article/ highlight workbooks	
8:35-8:45	8:39, 8:43	Content	Polling	A-E multiple choice
8:45-8:50	8:47	Content	Text chat	Quick question/ response
8:50-8:52	8:50	Evaluation	Polling	Pre-made questions

Figure 11.1

Poor Pacing

Many facilitators and trainers are focused on flow, timing, and other details, and it is easy to forget to check-in with learners to find out if they are comfortable with the level of detail and ready to move on. Teach learners at the beginning how to use their pacing tools and give them permission to ask that the session be sped up or slowed down. Pause the session occasionally to ask how the pace is for the learners. This will give you a pulse and give learners a chance to feel comfortable giving feedback. If a majority of the group wants to slow down, slow down. If only one person is regularly asking for a quicker pace, consider giving them additional tasks like being a team scribe or time keeper. This will help keep them engaged while others take notes or problem solve.

Too Many People Talking at Once
When using VoIP, there can be a lot of feedback when multiple users all have their microphones on. Practice calling on participants and having them raise their hands electronically to share; it will reduce the double voices and feedback for all. Have learners turn on their microphones when talking and turn them back off when they are finished. The producer can also help by turning off mics that were left on accidentally.

Too Much Text on Screen
PowerPoint puke is in the past. No more 700-word slides that are read. Slides should aid the presenter, not be the presenter. This rule applies to pre-made slides, not the slides participants create themselves. Instead of text, use images and photographs to depict ideas and concepts. In chapter six, there are a lot of examples and ideas on making your PowerPoint interactive and usable.

Using Too Many Tools
Just because a trainer knows how to use the tools doesn't mean all of them need to be used. It reminds me of a participant who went through The Bob Pike Group's Train-the-Trainer Boot Camp. She went back to work so excited that she decided to test everything out and amazingly implemented more than 30 ideas in a 30-minute meeting. Her company culture was used to lectures, and the interactive culture shock was over the top. Implementing one or two ideas would have been better. As learners got used to those engagement techniques, she could have added a few more or tried something different. Pretty soon the group buys into the interaction because the change is gradual.

Online is the same way. Just because a trainer knows the platform doesn't mean the learners do. Overuse tools and the session becomes a juggling act. Juggling one ball or two balls is manageable for all, but, as more balls are added, it becomes more difficult and nearly impossible for those of us who haven't learned the skill. More time is spent trying to get participants up to speed on where to find tools than it is on the actual content itself.

Not Practicing
Winging it won't work. If someone hasn't practiced the webinar, it typically becomes an online lecture. To avoid this, plan what tools you want to use during each of the activities and energizers. Give thought

to the steps, and practice pulling up each of the tools and giving clear directions. Think through how many participants will text chat or whiteboard at a time and what to do if they write on top of one another. Take the time to be confident with the tools. It provides more flexibility for the session and also makes the webinar more seamless.

Lecture, Lecture, Lecture

Death by lecture (also the title of a good book by Sharon Bowman) is one way to kill motivation. Instead, build in interactive learning activities from this book. Test out one interaction and see how things go. If you aren't enthusiastic about the activities, the participants won't be either, so begin with the exercises that are easiest and more your style. "I have to lecture," some might say. I am a recovering lecturer as well, and here you can start down the road to recovery. Admitting it is the first step.

Here are a few ideas to get you started:

- Break up lectures into smaller 4-minute lecturettes,
- Have participants be guest presenters on content they have expertise in,
- Use a short video clip to teach a section,
- Allow for learners to digest information by jotting down action ideas in their workbooks,
- Ask questions throughout the lecture and have learners text chat; use their examples and ideas.

Appearing (or Being) Disorganized

If learners think the facilitator is clueless or disorganized, credibility is lost and hard to regain. Be consistent in where you place items you will use. If demonstrating the use of props on the webcam, have them readily available on the desk. If sharing a link to a website, check the link the morning of the session and have it ready to paste in. When application sharing your desktop, be sure to clear or file miscellaneous documents and shortcuts not needed for the session. The appearance of organization goes a long way, and it does help in maintaining an organized session and platform.

Improper Handling of Questions

The purpose of a question in an online webinar is for learning to take place, not testing. Most sessions I have attended either run out of time or spend too much time on one question. If the answer goes beyond the 4 minutes, I'm not listening; I'm queuing my movies on Netflix.

Allow participants time to process or craft questions in sub groups. This increases the buy-in for all and eliminates questions that are not valid or can be answered by another learner. Allow learners to "ask three before you ask me" when it comes to content that has already been covered. This encourages other learners to adapt and assimilate the information enough to help bring another up to speed.

No Evaluation
Smiley sheets and feedback forms are used in the classroom on a regular basis but when it comes to online training, they are nowhere to be found. In webinars where I've been an attendee, more than 65 percent of the facilitators didn't have any type of evaluation at any point during their session. How do they know if I was bored and not participating? How will they know if several concepts were over my head? They won't. They may feel like they did a great job because 50 people logged in initially, but when I log out at the end of the session, there may be only 11 left in the room. After only a few minutes, participants not paying for a webinar will log out if it isn't worth their investment of time. Keep them engaged and ask for feedback to make the next session even better.

Deadly Sins Committed by Producers
The producer is the person who takes care of many technical and logistical responsibilities before, during, and after a webinar. This person offers invaluable assistance to the trainer and makes sure that everything gets taken care of behind the scenes so that the trainer can focus on the material and the participants. During the course of the webinar, there are several things that the producer should pay attention to and simply take care of as they happen. When it doesn't happen, then it becomes a deadly sin. This list describes a lot of the roles and responsibilities of the producer.

Not Showing Up
Having the producer be a no-show has happened, and when a trainer is expecting support but doesn't receive it, he starts off baffled and needs to overcome angst and a raw set of nerves while trying to juggle an even

larger number of tasks. A producer must be reliable and on time or early. Not showing up for the session until it is almost over can be disastrous to the class, especially if there are several tasks to be done.

Not Opening the Teleconference
Not only should the teleconference line be opened well in advance of learners logging on, but the producer should also know how to turn it on quickly should VoIP go out. Having a learner request it because of bandwidth issues and not being able to successfully connect them is deadly for all. Plan ahead for practicing this amidst a session and in the moment. If you haven't had to do this in awhile, a quick refresher is a good idea.

Not Testing Media Ahead of Time
It is the producer's responsibility to log in early and make sure slides are loaded and working properly as well as any other media that may be used for the session. Planning ahead and doing a little bit of technical troubleshooting saves a lot of time and headaches later.

Not Knowing the Platform
The producer is a technical resource and should know the platform and technology well enough that she can answer basic questions and do minor troubleshooting for the different tools. Each platform has its own user guide; the producer should have a copy of this and be ready to provide answers quickly. When a producer isn't able to quickly put up a timer or get people swiftly into breakout rooms, technology begins to take center stage instead of the content. She should also be able to assign tool permissions and set up breakout rooms in advance. It also means having Information Technology (IT) and the support number for the platform on speed dial.

Forgetting to Record
When a session needs to be recorded for future replay, and the producer forgets to engage the recorder, this could be a problem for everyone. I recommend starting the recording before the session starts and letting it go for the entire length of the session. You can edit out any unnecessary breaks later.

I once paused a recording for a break in an effort to save on editing time; however, I forgot to start it again and this "shortcut" ended up backfiring.

Lesson learned. Planning to edit is better than not having anything to edit at all.

Not Answering Text Chat Questions

Participants need attention when they have questions. If the question was posted to the group, but scrolls off the screen before the trainer has a chance to respond, the producer should privately text chat the trainer the identical question. If a learner privately text chats the producer, the producer should respond to that question in kind.

Text questions are like being on hold; check back in from time to time and give a status update so learners don't think you have forgotten them. Once when I was producing, a question was posed to me. I did not know the answer, so I began to search quickly for a response. In the meantime, the person texted me again; I hadn't bothered to let him know what I was doing the first time. So this time, I did respond with what I was doing and told him I would get back to him in just a minute or two.

Unresponsive to Participant and Instructor Needs

If participants do not come back from break or lunch, give them a call or send an email to make sure that everything is okay. When a producer doesn't respond to learner needs, it reflects directly on the trainer and the class as a whole. In the evaluation, there should be one or two questions related to the producer and his ability as well as his attitude toward helping participants.

Lacking Initiative

If a producer needs to be micromanaged and has to get specific, detailed directions for everything, it adds another level of stress for the facilitator. A producer should be self-directed and reliable. When there is something that needs to be taken care of, the producer is the go-to person. If the trainer's sound fails and he needs to leave the room and log back in, the producer should be ready to jump in and get learners into an activity so that it isn't a big deal and time is not wasted on waiting.

Not Staying Focused

Some might believe producing is a cushy job because there is so much free time in-between producer tasks. MISTAKE! A producer should be keeping track of timing, saving screenshots for future reference, adding to notations on the whiteboard, saving whiteboard slides, helping learners with their tools for whiteboarding, or setting up polling among other tasks the trainer has requested.

When a producer gets side tracked, she begins to miss cues for breakout rooms, not paste notes on the whiteboard or in the text chat area, have late or absent application launches, and neglect answering questions. Playing video games and ordering swimsuits are not part of the producer's task list. She needs to put away the smart phone and take good notes to share with the facilitator after the session.

Deadly Sins Committed by Managers

Managers play a big role in whether learning occurs or not. If a manager chooses not to let an employee participate in the webinar, then nothing can be learned or transferred back to the job. The manager's role in a webinar is to provide a safe environment for their employees to take the class, support the process, and help minimize distractions surrounding the employees while the webinar is going. It also means providing the support for systems and firewalls to be working so they can be successful. However, there are several things a manager can do to destroy the learning process for a webinar participant. Here are a few of a manager's deadly sins:

Putting Down the Class

Sharing negative opinions about the content or the trainer and making the employee feel dumb for even attending can kill any positive job-based outcome from the webinar. The session hasn't even begun and already the employee doesn't want to be there. This makes the trainer's job more difficult because now there are additional barriers, beyond technology, to overcome.

Interrupting

Receiving 10 emails in the first half hour all marked high priority removes the participant from the classroom. It's like knocking on the door of the training room 10 times and asking to speak to the same employee. Just because the class is online and the learner has access to email doesn't mean he is available to answer or respond. An interactive class keeps a learner working and learning all throughout with little time to respond to vague emergencies.

Not Following Up
After the session, managers seem to rarely follow up to discuss an ongoing action plan or ideas on how to implement the learning. This is a mistake because it doesn't encourage the learner to action plan. In fact, it promotes passive participation because there isn't accountability for having learned anything anyway.

Hovering
Being a helicopter manager doesn't make learning the content easier. Walking by the employee's office too many times makes him conscious he is being watched, which increases his tension, decreases retention, and reduces his participation on the webinar. Stay away and give them space to breath, kick back, and enjoy the process of learning online. Don't ask why he is shooting baskets into imaginary trash cans; just know it is all part of the learning process.

Having Multiple Participants Share Technology
Saving a few bucks and having a group interact as one person can take away from their online experience. Having one person "drive" while the others sit back isn't fun and doesn't enhance learning; allow learners to be individuals and take the class for themselves. Let them draw on their own whiteboards and talk in their own breakout rooms. The ability to learn the material is largely connected to those interactions and application.

Deadly Sins Committed by Learners
Learners are responsible for their own engagement, focus, ability to learn, and self-motivation. They walk in with prior knowledge, skills, and abilities that can help the classroom thrive and become a catalyst for learning. Participants should come prepared to learn and discover with open minds. Here are some of the biggest sins I have encountered.

Johnny Come Lately
Technology takes time to boot up and log into, not to mention the added delays of server speeds and streaming. If a trainer has decided to stream a video and a song or two, that will slow learners' log in. Encourage them to log in at least 15 minutes before and get the audio setup done before going to get another cup of caffeine. Logging in late is even worse because now they have missed all the tool practice and are lost or are using up valuable producer time to get up to speed.

The Socializer
Sending private texts and being sarcastic or inappropriate is a webinar no-no. This can be prevented by setting ground rules and expectations as a group ahead of time. Most people want to do the right thing, but that is hard to do if they don't have clear rules to guide them. Peers will hold one another accountable so the trainer and producer don't have to. Be sure to switch up breakout rooms so that the socializers don't exhaust their peers.

The Disengaged or Unresponsive
When attending a class that is participant-centered, the one individual who doesn't poll, add a thought, raise a hand, or share can be a nightmare. The producer needs to connect with this person. Ask a question like, "It appears your tool bar isn't working; is there something I can help you with?" Once they know you have noticed them, it is surprising how they come to life.

Another trick is to choose team leaders to help with tasks. You can choose team leaders by telling them it is the person who raises a hand last or not at all!

The Complainer
When participants consistently find things wrong with your webinar—the music you play, the tools being used, the questions asked—they are focusing on the wrong things, creating a distraction for the facilitator and producer, and eating up valuable connecting time while sucking the life out of you. They may also be taking away from their peers' ability to learn, depending on how they are sharing the feedback. When this sin arises, gently ask them to refrain from sharing feedback, but let them know there will be an opportunity for feedback at the end.

The Distracted
The learner who logs in and then walks away from the computer to run errands, take a shower, yell at kids or bathe their dog is distracted. Clients have come to The Bob Pike Group asking me what they can do to get these things to stop. One client shared that a participant got her kids ready, yelled at them to hurry up, swore as the milk spilled on the floor and so on for 35 minutes. There were 200 people on the webinar, and there was no way to mute her phone on the conference call. If a participant-centered class has engagement every 4 minutes, these distractions become less frequent.

CHAPTER TWELVE

Types of Interactivities and How to Use Them

You never get a second chance to make a good first impression. How you handle log-in difficulties, open the webinar, or help those struggling to get up to speed all impact each learner's first impression of your online training session.

A participant-centered webinar uses different types of interactions to help make the first, last, and every impression along the way positive and lasting. By utilizing CLOSER (Closers, Learning activities, Openers, Soft openers, Energizers and Revisiters), you are choosing to put WOW Factor into your webinars. Participants aren't used to being engaged through entire webinars. When they experience an interactive one with better recall of the material covered, they leave delighted and look more positively toward the next one.

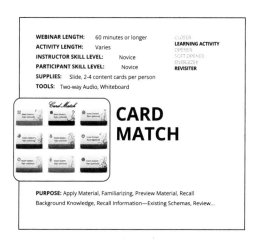

The last section of this book lays out more than 40 activities you can do in a webinar to keep people engaged and motivated while still focusing on your content. Following is a brief tutorial on what the purpose of each part of CLOSER is so you can easily select the right activities from the last chapter for your content segments.

Closers

Think about the last webinar you were on. What were the last five minutes like? Did the instructor do a question-and-answer time? Did it go long? Did the instructor ask for an evaluation to be filled out?

The last few minutes of a session is prime real estate and should be used to solidify information and brand it on the brain. People should walk away knowing what their next action step is and how to get started.

A closer can be motivational and inspirational. Closers revisit the content and bring things full circle. They are a chance to celebrate and rejoice in the learning and be proud of what has been accomplished. If learners walk away feeling poorly about how much they don't know, we have done a great disservice to them.

The course evaluation should not be part of the closer. Evaluations should be done about three-fourths of the way through the training so the last minutes can be focused on the learners and what they are taking away.

When selecting a closer, pick one that suits the time frame—the shorter the class, the shorter the closer. I usually have a backup closer just in case I was planning on having 10 minutes, but now we are down to 3 minutes. Even in 3 minutes, I can do a quick whiteboard close. There are several ideas in this book that are shorter in time frame and others can be modified for a quicker close as well.

Learning Activity

Many instructional designers find it easy to adapt to using an opener and a closer; however, most find it challenging to take the content and make it more interactive. Learning activities are the interactive framework on which to hang your content.

For example, a learning frame could be as simple as using a card match or sort. Take a section of your information, like a step-by-step process. Create cards with the information on them, with one complete or partial step per card. Have six to 12 cards per slide, then have learners review the deck and highlight what they think goes first. When someone has identified and explained what additional information is needed, move on to the next. Instead of a bulleted PowerPoint lecture, the content has become active, and learners are engaged as they automatically want to know if their guess or deduction was right.

While learning through these activities usually takes longer than a lecture, they also incorporate case studies, brainstorming and information application. Learning activities are the "lecture" because you are teaching as you go through the activity.

Openers

When starting a training session, you need to first break learner preoccupation for your information to have the best chance of sticking. Openers are your first line of offense for this task.

Openers can serve many purposes, including creating an atmosphere of collegiality. These activities get people into the room, get them networking, and make the session feel more like a real class and not just solitary confinement. They can decrease tension in a group and provide a safe way to practice using the tools and talking with others. When one person begins sharing, others feel more comfortable opening up. Soon all participants are text chatting, and there is a bit of relief as tool-usage confidence is built as are relationships. Openers lay the groundwork for participation throughout the rest of the webinar.

The length of the opener depends on the amount of content used and the length of the session. If there are four 3-hour modules, I will spend about 30 minutes opening the first day to lay the foundation for a safe environment. This way, when I later engage them in a rather off-the-wall energizer, the participants participate as I model the exercise via my webcam.

As you read through the different interactivities at the end of this book, some can be used as the opener or closer because they meet the principles of both.

Soft Openers

Soft openers help warm up the brain and get it going. Strong soft openers will encourage lateral thinking, meaning it is both creative and logical, requiring both sides of the brain to come up with a solution. Good soft openers should tie into the content but not be need-to-know. They are meant to be an add-on and should transition into the opener. They should also be simple and allow for all learners to join in.

Soft openers are typically started 5 to 10 minutes before beginning the webinar and engage the audience, set the tone, put attendees at ease, and allow learners to begin practicing the platform tools.

My producer and I welcome people as they enter the session and have them chat with us for a minute. A warm welcome with a question after is a simple way to break the ice and start a conversation. Then we'll start the soft opener.

If the group is new to one another, use the soft opener to connect people or find out what they already know about the training topic. If the participants are from all different levels of the organization, you could use the soft opener to level out the playing field—no matter what role each learner has, all are equal when it comes to whiteboarding how you feel right now or text chatting a solution to a puzzle.

The soft opener ideas in this book just need your content. I typically finish up the final soft opener about 3 minutes into the session so everyone can finish logging in. I then move into the opener. Soft openers only occur prior to the start of a session. They are not mandatory, but they are part of what creates a WoW Factor.

Energizers

When you are feeling tired, your learners are as well. Do a quick energizer and watch yourself transform! You and your learners will feel better.

Energizers are activities that get the blood flowing and help participants refocus. If you don't have a few energizers ready and planned into your webinar, they are unlikely to happen. The most useful times for energizers in a webinar tend to be after a large section of content or application practice around the 60-minute mark. If you are hosting a webinar after lunch, a quick break about 20 minutes into your session is a good time to get people back on their feet for a physical energizer to increase blood flow and oxygen for optimal brain function and learning.

Energizers are the one type of activity that do not have to specifically relate to the content. Energizers are meant to be a rapid way to get learners re-engaged. The energizers in this book are 1 to 5 minutes.

When you decide to use a longer energizer, consider a revisiter that has a kinesthetic component.

Revisiters

What on earth is a revisiter and is it contagious? A revisit activity is similar to a review in that it goes over content already covered; however, review is where the instructor goes over the material again. A revisit is where the learner goes over the material. Some of the main differences between the two are listed in Figure 12.1. There is a time and place for both, but a revisiter will usually benefit the learner more and provide a growing action plan.

CONVENTIONAL REVIEW	PARTICIPANT-CENTERED REVISIT
Announce the review	Don't announce, just do it
Trainer does a summary	Learners summarize
Specific right or wrong answers	Flexible answers
Conceptual in nature [This is how it will work]	Behavioral [This is how I will apply it]
Test based	Journal and internal discovery
Fixed structure	Unstructured
Measurable	More difficult to measure
Examples: PowerPoint review slides, verbal review, reading review, observation with note taking, theoretical work	Examples: Physical activity, games and exercises, actually doing the job or task with a job aid, teaching others, top takeaway, brainstorming/journaling

Figure 12.1

Chapter 13 is designed to save trainers time by providing easy, ready-to-use exercises. These exercises are cross-referenced in the index. Keep in mind that activity lengths can last longer than the length specified depending on the number of participants, complexity of the content, and the amount of application time a trainer wants to provide.

Most exercises require a slide be made in advance; however, it is better to be using the exercises, even if you don't have time to create the appropriate slide using PowerPoint design principles for webinars.

Each of the activities in this book also has a slide created with the design principles in mind. To save time and avoid slide-design frustration, these slides can be purchased at store.bobpikegroup.com/music-and-media for about the price of a good Chicago-style pizza.

Congratulations on taking steps to make your webinars more engaging. I look forward to seeing you in a live online session!

Good luck and God bless,

Becky Pluth

CHAPTER THIRTEEN
Interactivities

WEBINAR LENGTH: Any
ACTIVITY LENGTH: 10-15 minutes
INSTRUCTOR SKILL LEVEL: Novice
PARTICIPANT SKILL LEVEL: Intermediate
SUPPLIES: Slide
TOOLS: Group Whiteboard, Two-way Audio

CLOSER
LEARNING ACTIVITY
OPENER
SOFT OPENER
ENERGIZER
REVISITER

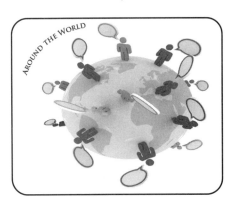

AROUND THE WORLD

Purpose
Brainstorm, Establish a Learning Community, Familiarizing, Recall Background Knowledge, Recall Information—Existing Schemas, Refocus Learner, Revisit

Setup
- Create a slide that includes the following:
  o Title: Around the World
  o Insert faint colorful watermark image of nature or the world
- Insert the slide(s) into the presentation at the appropriate place based on your purpose: in the beginning as an opener, partway through the webinar if used as a revisiter, or before a break or at the very end of the session if used as a closer. If used as a learning activity, insert the slide when the content comes up in the presentation.

Trainer Process

- Put up the "Around the World" slide.
- Have each participant write their name on the whiteboard in a color that will show up against the background.
- Each participant will have a turn to share on the topic you name. It could be a best learning, step in a process, or a solution to a problem.
- Virtually hand the highlighter to a first participant, and tell them you're handing off the koosh ball. They will share a first idea and "toss" the virtual koosh ball to another name on the whiteboard by drawing a line from their name to another.
- This continues until everyone has shared.

Producer Process

- In a document, keep track of brainstorming ideas shared.
- Help learners with tools and drawing lines if needed.
- Make sure microphones are muted after each share.

Variations

- In a hurry? Sometimes drawing the line takes up a bit of time. Use a pointing tool instead of the highlighter and point at the next person to share.
- Shorten the activity by allowing learners to only share one word or one sentence before passing the koosh.

WEBINAR LENGTH: Any
ACTIVITY LENGTH: 5 minutes
INSTRUCTOR SKILL LEVEL: Intermediate
PARTICIPANT SKILL LEVEL: Intermediate
SUPPLIES: Slide
TOOLS: Group Whiteboard

CLOSER
LEARNING ACTIVITY
OPENER
SOFT OPENER
ENERGIZER
REVISITER

ATZRR
(A TO Z RELAY RACE)

Purpose
Brainstorm, Establish a Learning Community, Familiarizing, Recall Background Knowledge, Recall Information—Existing Schemas, Refocus Learner, Revisit

Setup
- Create a handout titled "Top Takeaways" for participants to write down learnings throughout the webinar.
- Create a slide that includes the following:
  o A to Z Relay
  o Split the slide into two halves with the letters A-M running vertically down the left hand side and the letters N-Z down the middle of the page with one letter per line. All the letters of the alphabet (English or otherwise) should be listed out.
- Insert the slide(s) into the presentation at the appropriate place based on your purpose: in the beginning as an opener, part-way through the webinar if used as a revisiter or, if used as a closer, before a break or at the very end of the session.

Trainer Process

- Have learners turn to their "Top Takeaways" page.
- Put up the "A to Z Relay" slide.
- Split group into two teams.
- Each team member will select a different color for writing. Players must alternate. For example, the learner who writes down an action idea must then wait for a teammate to post another idea before they may post again. Thus the relay!
- Learners will fill in each letter with a learning point from the session. In a customer service class you might see S=Smile on the phone, X=Xtra time with elderly, etc. Share that creative spelling counts!
- When a group is done, all participants raise their virtual hands, and the game is over!
- Before starting the relay, ask if anything needs clarifying.
- Check in on participants in their breakout rooms during the relay (variation only).
- When completed, discuss the ideas as a large group.
- Direct learners to add ideas to their "Top Takeaways" page.
- Have learners then circle their favorite idea posted on the whiteboard.

Producer Process

- Put up a timer for 30, 45 or 60 seconds and have it count down (variation only).
- Post A to Z slide in breakout rooms (variation only).
- After groups are done, post the winning slide in the main room (variation only).

Variations

- If the class is small enough, you can work as a large group on the main room whiteboard.
- If a large group, put the A to Z chart in each breakout room and race against other breakout rooms to finish the entire chart first. The team that finishes first and raises their hands wins.
- If it is a small group, make it a race against the clock.
- If it is a small group, have one team work on the first half of the alphabet while the other group works on the second half.

Webinars with WOW Factor

WEBINAR LENGTH: Any
ACTIVITY LENGTH: 10-15 minutes
INSTRUCTOR SKILL LEVEL: Advanced
PARTICIPANT SKILL LEVEL: Intermediate
SUPPLIES: Slide, Hyperlink for Response Pads
TOOLS: Application Share, Two-way Audio, Virtual Response Pad

CLOSER
LEARNING ACTIVITY
OPENER
SOFT OPENER
ENERGIZER
REVISITER

BRAVO!™
WITH PING™ VIRTUAL RESPONSE SYSTEM

Purpose

Apply Material, Brainstorm, Combining, Establish a Learning Community, Familiarizing, Innovate New Ideas, Introduce New Concept, Preview Material, Recall Background Knowledge, Recall Information—Existing Schemas, Refocus Learner, Revisit, Teach New Material

Setup

- Purchase BRAVO! With PING software or download a trial license for free at C3Softworks.com
- Select an interactive game that suits the content. All the games are colorful and fully customizable. For fun, create a custom avatar that looks like the president of the company as one of the contestants.
- Create and test the game.
- Insert PING link into leader's guide for quick reference.
- Create a slide that includes the following:
    o Image of the launch page and image of the response pad.
    o Directions on how the game works. This will vary based on the exercise selected by the facilitator.
    o Link to the PING pad.

Trainer Process

- Put up the slide of the image and directions for learners.
- Split learners into groups based on the number of teams desired.
- Launch BRAVO! game on facilitator desktop to get ready for application share.
- Have learners click on the hyperlink. Let them know a new window will open when they click on the link. This new window can be moved around so that they are still able to see the facilitator's screen and platform.
- Once the window pops up, click on the Launch button.
- Wait for learners while they do this.
- Have learners select their team and enter their name.
- Watch as learners' names begin to ring in. Once all have rung in, start application-sharing the game.
- Start the game and ask the questions. Have participants ring in with their virtual PING pads.
- Continue getting answers to game questions until the game is done.
- Stop application sharing and have learners text chat learnings from the exercise.

Producer Process

- Help participants get up and running with the PING virtual pads.
- Monitor text chat area while game is in play.

Variations

- Application share BRAVO! without the PING pads and have learners raise their hand or text chat the letter as their response.
- Have learners go through their own version by giving them a link to the game. They can then play the game alone and at any time.

WEBINAR LENGTH: > 90 minutes
ACTIVITY LENGTH: 20-30 minutes
INSTRUCTOR SKILL LEVEL: Advanced
PARTICIPANT SKILL LEVEL: Advanced
SUPPLIES: Slide
TOOLS: Breakout Rooms, Group Whiteboard

CLOSER
LEARNING ACTIVITY
OPENER
SOFT OPENER
ENERGIZER
REVISITER

BURSTING BALLOONS

Purpose
Apply Material, Combining, Establish a Learning Community, Familiarizing, Innovate New Ideas, Introduce New Concept, Preview Material, Recall Background Knowledge, Recall Information—Existing Schemas, Refocus Learner, Revisit, Teach New Material

Setup
- Create a handout titled "Top Takeaways" for participants to write down learnings throughout the webinar.
- Create a slide that includes the following:
  o Title: Bursting Balloons
  o An image in the background of multicolored balloons that are labeled with topics covered in the session.
  o "Team moderator is the person wearing the most colors."
- Insert the slide(s) into the presentation at the appropriate place based on your purpose: in the beginning as an opener, partway through the webinar if used as a revisiter or, if used as a closer, before a break or at the very end of the session.

Becky Pike Pluth, M.Ed., CSP

Trainer Process
- Have learners turn to their "Top Takeaways" page.
- Put up the "Bursting Balloons" slide.
- Split the group into two teams.
- Teams will be put into breakout rooms to write concepts on the whiteboard that relate to each topic on the balloons.
- Demonstrate by writing an idea on the whiteboard.
- Set the timer for 2 minutes. Encourage learners to list as many ideas on their whiteboards as they can for each topic.
- After 2 minutes, teams will highlight their top two ideas and meet back in the main room.
- Ask, "What questions can I answer regarding this activity?"
- Send groups into their assigned breakout rooms for 2 minutes.
- Return teams to the main room.
- If using as an opener, do this as a large group. Have learners list things they already know about the topics to be covered today.
- Have the team leader share the two best ideas with the large group. No repeats.
- Have participants add to their "Top Takeaways" page in their workbooks while groups are sharing.

Producer Process
- Create breakout rooms.
- Post the "Bursting Balloons" slide in each breakout room.
- Send learners into their breakout rooms.
- Put up a timer for 2 minutes and have it count down.
- Check in on breakout rooms and answer any questions.
- Post breakout room whiteboards into the main room for viewing or application share the whiteboards.
- Tally the number of points each team receives and post the score on their slide.

Variations
- If it is a small group, each participant can be on their own team or work as a large group to achieve a certain score in 2 minutes.
- If working on a platform that allows for animation, create hyperlinks and allow learners to click on a balloon, which will then reveal the topic. Groups can share via text chat what they have learned.

Webinars with WOW Factor

WEBINAR LENGTH: 60 minutes or longer
ACTIVITY LENGTH: Varies
INSTRUCTOR SKILL LEVEL: Novice
PARTICIPANT SKILL LEVEL: Novice
SUPPLIES: Slide, Two to Four Content Cards Per Person
TOOLS: Two-way Audio, Whiteboard

CLOSER
LEARNING ACTIVITY
OPENER
SOFT OPENER
ENERGIZER
REVISITER

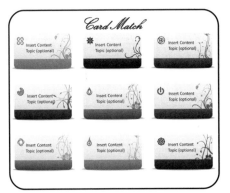

CARD MATCH

Purpose
Apply Material, Familiarizing, Preview Material, Recall Background Knowledge, Recall Information—Existing Schemas, Revisit

Setup
- Prior to the session, create a deck of cards. Each card should be labeled with a piece of content covered in this session. Content could include terms or images depending on the session material.
- Determine the number of cards each person will receive. This can vary from two to four random cards per learner.
- If there are not enough content pieces for unique cards for each learner, you can repeat content cards as needed.
- Email or mail each participant two to four random cards (you may want to keep track of who received what pieces).
- Create "Card Match" revisit slide(s) that include the following:
  o Title: "Card Match" with image of playing cards or the scanned-in cards that were created.
  o The content of the slide(s) should match the cards created. For example, content could include terms or images depending on the session material.

- Insert pre-made "Card Match" revisit slide(s) in several places throughout the deck after a few content pieces have been covered. This is roughly every 20 minutes.

Trainer Process

- At the beginning of the session, have participants open their cards and read or view their cards.
- Explain that each card correlates to content to be covered. At certain points along the way, you will stop and do a "card match." This is when anyone who has a card with a topic that was covered will raise their hand and share one thing they learned on the topic or how they plan to adapt, adopt, and apply what they learned back on the job.
- Learners should take notes on their cards as the content is covered and be ready to share.
- Put up the "Card Match" slide.
- Have participants raise their hands if one of their cards has been covered.
- Call on each, one at a time, and have them share one thing they learned on that topic or how they plan to adapt, adopt, and apply what they learned back on the job.

Producer Process

- Participate as the radio show announcer reading the text chat or whiteboard ideas.

Variation

- To speed up this exercise, have learners who raised their hands to whiteboard or text chat their ideas and, as a talk-show host, "announce" their thoughts to the group or have another learner do so.
- If participants have prior knowledge or you want to include information learned in a prior session, add directions that some cards have content from the past sessions and that they can share how they have been applying it on the job.

WEBINAR LENGTH: > 30 minutes
ACTIVITY LENGTH: 2-5 minutes
INSTRUCTOR SKILL LEVEL: Novice
PARTICIPANT SKILL LEVEL: Novice
SUPPLIES: Slide
TOOLS: Group Whiteboard

CLOSER
LEARNING ACTIVITY
OPENER
SOFT OPENER
ENERGIZER
REVISITER

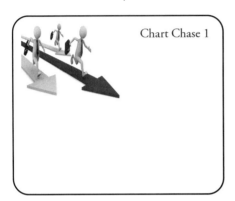

Chart Chase 1

CHART CHASE

Purpose
Apply Material, Brainstorm, Combining, Establish a Learning Community, Familiarizing, Innovate New Ideas, Introduce New Concept, Preview Material, Recall Background Knowledge, Recall Information—Existing Schemas, Refocus Learner, Revisit, Teach New Material

Setup
- Create a handout titled "Top Takeaways" for participants to write down learnings throughout the webinar.
- Create a slide that includes the following:
  o   Title: Chart Chase
- Insert the slide throughout for revisiting or, if used as a closer, before a break or the end.

Trainer Process
- Have learners turn to their "Top Takeaways" page.
- Put up the "Chart Chase" slide.
- Share that the group will have 30, 45 or 60 seconds to post as many learnings as possible. Select the time that best fits the number of ideas possible. The fewer the number of ideas, the shorter the time. Keep in mind some learners are slow typers. Learners new to the platform and using tools may also need more time. Assess the audience to determine the length of time.
- Post ideas on the whiteboard using the webinar platform tools (different colors, drawing tools, text, etc.).
- Duplicates do not count.
- The goal is to beat the last team's score. If this is the first time using this activity, have a goal of one to two ideas per person that are unique or take the number of learning points and divide by two. Don't be surprised by the number of unique ideas a group can generate in such a short amount of time.
- When time is up, pause the group by saying, "Time's up, pens up. It is now time to add ideas to your 'Top Takeaways' page while I [or learners] read the whiteboard ideas and count the number of unique ideas."
- Have learners then star their favorite idea so far.

Producer Process
- Put up a timer for 30, 45 or 60 seconds and have it count down.
- Answer any questions that come through via text chat.

Variations
- Do this several times throughout a session, trying to get the number posted higher and higher each time.
- Have learners post ideas on how to adapt the information to their work.
- Have learners post how they will adopt the information in the next month.

Webinars with WOW Factor

WEBINAR LENGTH: > 30 minutes
ACTIVITY LENGTH: 2-5 minutes
INSTRUCTOR SKILL LEVEL: Intermediate
PARTICIPANT SKILL LEVEL: Intermediate
SUPPLIES: Slide
TOOLS: Whiteboard and Drawing/Writing tools

CLOSER
LEARNING ACTIVITY
OPENER
SOFT OPENER
ENERGIZER
REVISITER

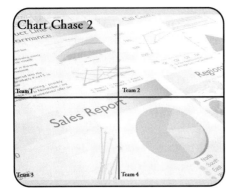

CHART CHASE 2

Purpose
Brainstorm, Combining, Establish a Learning Community, Familiarizing, Innovate New Ideas, Introduce New Concept, Preview Material, Recall Background Knowledge, Recall Information—Existing Schemas, Refocus Learner, Revisit, Teach New Material

Setup
- Create a handout titled "Top Takeaways" for participants to write down learnings throughout the webinar.
- Create a slide that includes the following:
  o Chart Chase 2
  o Split the slide into one quadrant per group; if there are only two groups, the slide will have a line down the middle creating a T. If there are four groups, it will look like a cross with four sections. Label each section Team 1, Team 2, etc.
- Insert the slides throughout for revisiting or before break or the end to be used as a closer.

Trainer Process
- Have learners turn to their "Top Takeaways" page.
- Put up the "Chart Chase 2" slide.
- Split participants into two or four groups. Label each group Team 1, Team 2, etc. A quick way to split into groups is alphabetically by first name.
- Share that the teams will have 30 seconds (or other appropriate amount of time) to post as many learnings as possible. If learners are new to the webinar platform, it would be best to begin with the activity titled "Chart Chase" to reduce frustration.
- Each team has a designated section where they will post ideas on the whiteboard using the webinar platform tools (different colors, drawing tools, text, etc.).
- Once an idea has been called out, it is "taken" and cannot be repeated. The facilitator will call out ideas as they are posted.
- Learners compete against other teams to post the most learning points in a given amount of time. You can keep a running tally of points to award prizes.
- When time is up, pause the group by saying, "Time's up, pens up. It is now time to add ideas to your 'Top Takeaways' page while I count the number of unique ideas."
- Have learners then highlight their favorite idea so far on the whiteboard.

Producer Process
- Put up a timer for the right amount of time and have it count down.
- Answer any questions that come through via text chat.
- Keep track of prize winners and send out awards.
- Ensure participants have permission to use their microphones or talk (variation only).

Variations
- They raise their hand, turn on their mics, and call out a topic and jot it in their space. Go in order of who raised their hand first.
- Keep a running tally of points throughout multiple session webinars and give away "bonus bucks" or online gift cards.
- Change up the award for the most ideas and keep your learners guessing.

WEBINAR LENGTH: > 90 minutes, multi-day
ACTIVITY LENGTH: 5-15 minutes
INSTRUCTOR SKILL LEVEL: Novice
PARTICIPANT SKILL LEVEL: Novice
SUPPLIES: Slide
TOOLS: Two-way Audio, Whiteboard

CLOSER
LEARNING ACTIVITY
OPENER
SOFT OPENER
ENERGIZER
REVISITER

CHECK AND BALANCE

Purpose
Applying Material, Combining, Revisit

Setup
- Create a "Top Takeaways" handout for the learners to add learnings to throughout the session.
- Create a "Check and Balance" slide that includes a picture of each participant or have each participant name listed.
- Insert the slide into the presentation at the end of the presentation as the final activity of the webinar.

Trainer Process
- Put up the "Check and Balance" slide.
- Have learners open their books to a "Top Takeaways" notes page and take 60 seconds to jot down ideas they want to be sure and use.
- After 60 seconds, begin a large group discussion by highlighting a learner's name.
- Have that person turn on their microphone and then share their learning and how they will use it.
- After they are done sharing, they will highlight another learner's name.
- The trick is that none of the learnings can be repeated! This is one way to evaluate whether the key points were caught and remembered.
- If a participant's top idea is "taken," they can move down their list and share a different idea.

Producer Process
- Put up timer for 60 seconds.
- Ensure learner microphone permissions are enabled.

Variations
- Have learners post their idea next to their name.
- Assign topic areas to groups of learners to focus on.
- Add additional theory after participants share as needed.

WEBINAR LENGTH: Any
ACTIVITY LENGTH: 10-15 minutes
INSTRUCTOR SKILL LEVEL: Novice
PARTICIPANT SKILL LEVEL: Novice
SUPPLIES: Slide
TOOLS: Text Chat

CLOSER
LEARNING ACTIVITY
OPENER
SOFT OPENER
ENERGIZER
REVISITER

CHIT CHAT

Purpose
Apply Material, Brainstorm, Familiarizing, Innovate New Ideas, Introduce New Concept, Recall Background Knowledge, Refocus Learner, Revisit

Setup
- Create a slide that includes the following:
  o Watermark image of people chatting.
  o Titled "Chit Chat" with the following information listed: "Using the chat or instant message tool bar, text chat one fact or learning on ___ [facilitator to select the topic.]" Examples: Text chat your number one takeaway. Text chat one thing you look forward to doing this weekend. Text Chat how you will apply principle X on the job.
  "Brainstorm different ways to use this information."
- Insert the slide into the presentation at any point as an energizer.

Trainer Process
- Put up the "Chit Chat" slide.
- Have learners stand up and stretch while they text chat the answer to the question.
- Turn on webcam to demonstrate standing up and model texting an idea.
- Once learners have finished answering, have them read through three other responses, and then take their seats.
- Read a few answers out loud and comment as participants are typing up their thoughts.
- Turn off webcam.
- If "Chit Chat" is content-related, have learners add two or three ideas to their "Top Takeaways" page or notes section.
- If "Chit Chat" is brainstorming, pick a couple of ideas and add content in the moment.

Producer Process
- Save the text chat at the end of the presentation.
- Assist learners with technical difficulties or questions.
- Put up timer for 2 minutes (variation only).

Variations
- Have learners private text chat one other person to share ideas.
- In a time crunch, put up a timer for 2 minutes and have learners text chat as many ideas as possible.
- Be specific about the content on which the learners should text chat.

WEBINAR LENGTH: Any
ACTIVITY LENGTH: 5 minutes
INSTRUCTOR SKILL LEVEL: Novice
PARTICIPANT SKILL LEVEL: Novice
SUPPLIES: Slide
TOOLS: Group Whiteboard

CLOSER
LEARNING ACTIVITY
OPENER
SOFT OPENER
ENERGIZER
REVISITER

DOUBLE TROUBLE!

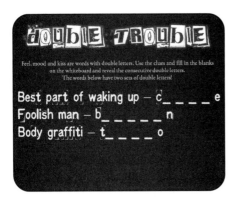

Purpose
Establish a Learning Community, Introduce New Concept, Refocus Learner

Setup
- Create a slide that includes the following (these can be split into individual slides):
    o   Title: Double Trouble
    o   "Feel," "mood" and "kiss" are words with double letters. Use the clues and fill in the blanks on the whiteboard and reveal the consecutive double letters. The words below have two sets of double letters!
        o   Best part of waking up — c_ _ _ _ e
        o   Foolish man — b_ _ _ _ _ n
        o   Body graffiti — t_ _ _ _ o
        o   Masked mammal — r_ _ _ _ _ n
        o   Describing a sheep — w_ _ _ _ y
        o   EXPERTS ONLY: try for this triple consecutive word — Systematic money recorder — b_ _ _ _ _ _ _ _ r

- Create a second slide that includes the answers:
  - Coffee
  - Buffoon
  - Tattoo
  - Raccoon
  - Woolly
  - Bookkeeper
- Insert the slide into the beginning of the presentation. Put up the slide prior to the webinar to help acclimate learners to the tools and to use as a soft opener. Insert at the beginning of the webinar if it is being used as an opener or anywhere throughout to be used as an energizer.

Trainer Process

- Put up the "Double Trouble" slide.
- Ask learners to place their guesses or ideas on the whiteboard.
- When someone has the right answer, move on to the next slide.
- When all have been solved, ask participants to make a connection between the double consecutive letters and what is being learned or will be learned.
  - Look for: sometimes we need to repeat ourselves, check and double check to make sure we've done the process correctly.
- No matter the riddle, it can be used as a quick way to energize a group and get brain cells firing again.

Producer Process

- Welcome participants as they enter the virtual room via text chat.

Variations

- Each learner is responsible for coming up with a word that has double letters. Post as many as possible in 90 seconds. Do the same for words with two and three sets of double letters. How does this relate to the content?
  - Look for: collaboration increases production; teamwork; the more consecutive letters you have, the harder it becomes to solve can be compared to the complexity of a process with more steps.
- Use easier words for quicker reaction and response. For more advanced critical thinkers, use slightly more complex words.
- Tie the word puzzle to the content whenever possible.
- Use the word puzzle to transition to a new topic.

WEBINAR LENGTH: Any
ACTIVITY LENGTH: 5-10 minutes
INSTRUCTOR SKILL LEVEL: Novice
PARTICIPANT SKILL LEVEL: Novice
SUPPLIES: Slide
TOOLS: Group Text Chat, Group Whiteboard

CLOSER
LEARNING ACTIVITY
OPENER
SOFT OPENER
ENERGIZER
REVISITER

FIND AND FIX

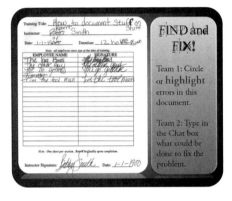

Purpose
Apply Material, Brainstorm, Combining, Familiarizing, Introduce New Concept, Recall Background Knowledge, Recall Information—Existing Schemas, Revisit

Setup
- Create a "Find and Fix" slide that includes the following:
  o A scanned-in form or document that has been incorrectly filled out. Examples of forms might be Good Manufacturing Practices (GMPs) or Standard Operating Procedures (SOPs).
  o A small text box with these directions
    - Group 1 — Highlight the errors
    - Group 2 — Text chat how the error can be fixed
- Insert the slide at the very beginning of the presentation as an opener, during a content piece to teach as a learning activity, after content is covered to revisit, as the last slide before break, or the end of the session to be used as a closer.

Trainer Process
- Put up the "Find and Fix" slide.
- Split group into two teams identified as Group 1 and Group 2.
    - Group 1 — Highlight the errors
    - Group 2 — Text chat how the error can be fixed
- Demonstrate how to highlight one error using the tools and fixed via the text chat.
- As errors are found, read off what was found and affirm or deny the error.
- If being used as a learning activity, pause the group at various points and talk about each of the errors and make improvements or additions to the thoughts posted.
- If Group 2 is struggling with how the error can be fixed, pause the groups and discuss options.

Producer Process
- During the demonstration, play the role of Group 2 and text chat how the error is fixed with the facilitator.
- Remove incorrect highlights.
- Put up timer (variation only).

Variations
- Time the "Find and Fix" and see how many errors can be found in the countdown against the clock!
- For large groups, put learners into breakout rooms in groups of four. Two participants work on the errors and two work on the resolution.
- Turn it into a group relay race where any learner can either highlight an error or correct an error that has been highlighted.

WEBINAR LENGTH: Any
ACTIVITY LENGTH: 5 minutes
INSTRUCTOR SKILL LEVEL: Novice
PARTICIPANT SKILL LEVEL: Novice
SUPPLIES: Slide
TOOLS: Two-way Audio, Group Whiteboard

CLOSER
LEARNING ACTIVITY
OPENER
SOFT OPENER
ENERGIZER
REVISITER

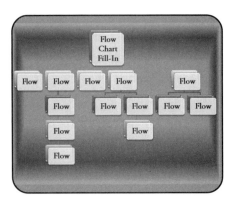

FLOW CHART FILL-IN

Purpose
Combining, Familiarizing, Preview Material, Recall Background Knowledge, Recall Information—Existing Schemas, Refocus Learner, Revisit, Teach New Material

Setup
- Create a "Flow Chart" slide that includes the following:
  - Image of a flow chart that includes the steps to a process that participants are learning about or have prior knowledge about.
  - Leave portions of the flow chart blank; participants will fill these in. The more the participants know about a process, the more blanks there should be. The more blanks, the more difficult.
- Insert the slide at the beginning of the session as an opener or at the end of the session as a closer. This slide can be used multiple times during a session. Fill it in as you go through each of the steps and enter the next phase of the flow chart.

Trainer Process

- Put up the "Flow Chart" slide.
- Allow 90 seconds for learners to fill in the blanks in the flow chart as a group.
- Areas that learners do not fill in help to identify gaps in their learning.
- Share with learners that all areas of the process will be covered, but more time will be spent covering topic areas that are weaker for the group.
- If this is being done as a closer, learners should fill in the blanks and then whiteboard one takeaway from the piece of the flow chart they filled in.
- If you are using this as a closer after content is learned, insert a blank flow chart, and have the group rotate filling in blanks and sharing learnings from each step of the process.

Producer Process

- Put up timer for 90 seconds.

Variations

- For large groups, do this in breakout rooms or select a smaller section of the group to write on the whiteboard.
- Insert the flow chart all throughout the session as a road map and insert as the group transitions from one portion of the flow chart to the next.
- Create a mind-map of content with blanks and have learners fill in the missing content pieces.
- If learners are new to the flow chart, add the flow chart topics on the page as a list and have learners work together and guess where they go in the process.

WEBINAR LENGTH: Any
ACTIVITY LENGTH: 1-5 minutes
INSTRUCTOR SKILL LEVEL: Novice
PARTICIPANT SKILL LEVEL: Novice
SUPPLIES: Slide
TOOLS: Polling

CLOSER
LEARNING ACTIVITY
OPENER
SOFT OPENER
ENERGIZER
REVISITER

FROZEN ACRONYMS

Purpose
Familiarizing, Introduce New Concept, Recall Background Knowledge, Recall Information—Existing Schemas, Refocus Learner, Revisit, Teach New Material

Setup
- Create a slide that includes the following:
  o Title: Frozen Acronyms
  o "Do selected motion in place for 30 seconds or until the facilitator calls out a new acronym. Freeze when you hear an acronym."
  o "Raise your online hand if you know what the acronym stands for."
- Create a slide that includes a list of activities:
  o Jumping
  o Jumping jacks
  o Stretching
  o Twisting
  o Playing air guitar
  o Free choice
- Insert the slide at the very beginning of the presentation as an opener, during a content piece to teach as a learning activity, after content is covered to revisit, or as the last slide before break or the end of the session to be used as a closer. Insert the slide anywhere throughout the presentation for fun as an energizer.

Trainer Process

- Put up the "Frozen Acronym" direction slide when learners are starting to fade.
- Have learners stand at their desks. Encourage participation by demonstrating the movements on a webcam.
- Put up the activity slide and have participants select an activity from the list.
- Participants should do the activity for 30 seconds or until the facilitator calls out an acronym at which point participants freeze.
- Remind the group to raise their hand if they know the definition.
- Facilitator calls on a volunteer to either define the acronym or use it in a sentence.
- Tell learners to resume their activity or begin a new activity when their peer has defined the acronym.
- After all listed ideas are done, ask participants to text chat how they are feeling now compared to before they took their break.

Producer Process

- Put on webcam and participate.
- Put up timer for 30 seconds. Reset and restart timer after each acronym.
- Post up ideas on whiteboard to get learners thinking (variation only).
- Keep track of team points (variation only).

Variations

- Have learners stand and text chat the definition or sentence. The first correct text chat gets a point for their team. Make teams fun—guys vs. gals, East Coast vs. West Coast, etc. Use multiple times with the second half of the session earning double points.
- In need of a quick, unplanned energizer? Put up a blank whiteboard and have learners post, one at a time, acronyms along with an exercise. Learners still define the acronym.
- Do as a timed activity; get through as many acronyms as possible in the allotted time. Keep track of how many you get through each time to see if the number defined improves.

WEBINAR LENGTH: Any
ACTIVITY LENGTH: Varies
INSTRUCTOR SKILL LEVEL: Novice
PARTICIPANT SKILL LEVEL: Novice
SUPPLIES: Slide
TOOLS: Whiteboard

CLOSER
LEARNING ACTIVITY
OPENER
SOFT OPENER
ENERGIZER
REVISITER

FULFILLING FILL-IN-THE BLANKS

Purpose
Apply Material, Brainstorm, Combining, Establish a Learning Community, Familiarizing, Innovate New Ideas, Introduce New Concept, Preview Material, Recall Background Knowledge, Recall Information—Existing Schemas, Refocus Learner, Revisit, Teach New Material

Setup
- Create learner handouts that have blanks in several places during a piece of content.
- Create slides that include the answers to the blanks in their handouts. The fill-in-the-blank word should be highlighted and underlined.
    o On the slide, put title: Fulfilling Fill-in-the-Blanks
    o A sample slide could read:
        - Make **bullet points** visual.
- Insert the slide wherever the content falls initially, at the start of the second day of a webinar if it is to be used as a revisiting opener, or partway through the webinar if used as a revisiter.

Trainer Process
- Have learners join you in their workbooks on the correct page.
- Begin lecturette and have learners fill in the blanks as the slides move along.
- Half-way through, have learners start or highlight in their workbooks the points that are most valuable to them.
- Continue through the slides until the section is complete.

Producer Process
- Text chat the correct words as they come up.

Variations
- If using two-way audio, have participants share their biggest takeaways from that section.
- Like competition? Have the fill-in answers at the bottom of the page and have learners guess what words fill in the blanks. Put up a timer for 90 seconds and see how many they can get.
- Put fill-in words on a slide and have learners share out loud what goes where. As they get one, share more about that piece of content or concept.

WEBINAR LENGTH: > 60 minutes, multi-day
ACTIVITY LENGTH: 5-10 minutes
INSTRUCTOR SKILL LEVEL: Novice
PARTICIPANT SKILL LEVEL: Novice
SUPPLIES: Slide
TOOLS: Group Text Chat

CLOSER
LEARNING ACTIVITY
OPENER
SOFT OPENER
ENERGIZER
REVISITER

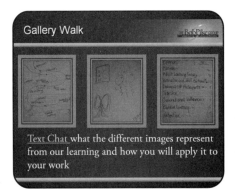

GALLERY RECOGNITION
GALLERY GUESSING

Purpose
Apply Material, Combining, Familiarizing, Introduce New Concept, Preview Material, Recall Background Knowledge, Recall Information—Existing Schemas, Refocus Learner, Revisit

Setup
- Create a "Gallery Recognition" slide that includes images that represent concepts or ideas in the session (it could be a symbol or number that also represents important data to the topic).
- Insert the slide into the presentation at the beginning of the day as a soft opener (see variation), start of the second day of a webinar to be used as a revisiting opener, partway through the webinar if used as a revisiter for that day's content or, if used as a closer, before a break or at the very end of the session.

Trainer Process
- Put up the "Gallery Recognition" slide.
- Have learners text chat the name of an image and what it represents from content learned or how it might relate to the topics of the day. Each learner will take a turn and rotate on to the next.
- Demonstrate to the class by text chatting an example. For example, if you have an image of "$," text the following: Dollar signs=increase revenue 2x in next 5 months or reduce spending by recycling.
- After text chatting an idea, the image can be highlighted or circled on the whiteboard. In smaller groups, this ensures all areas have been revisited.
- After all items are highlighted or circled, stop participants and instruct them to read back through the text chat and what others have written.
- If used as a closer, have learners write down ideas on the "Top Takeaways" page or notes section.

Producer Process
- Put up a timer for 1-3 minutes and have it count down (variation only).
- Save the text chat at the end of the presentation.

Variations
- In small groups, assign an image to each participant.
- In larger groups, refrain from highlighting and circling, assuming that each one will be touched on with all of the learners.
- In a time crunch, put up a timer for 2 minutes and have learners text chat on as many ideas as possible.
- In "Gallery Guessing," the learners only have an idea of course content and must try to make sense and meaning of the images. This could be used as a soft opener to begin generating ideas about what is to come. In this situation, there may be more than one correct interpretation.

WEBINAR LENGTH: Any
ACTIVITY LENGTH: 5-10 minutes
INSTRUCTOR SKILL LEVEL: Novice
PARTICIPANT SKILL LEVEL: Novice
SUPPLIES: Slide
TOOLS: Breakout Rooms, Group Whiteboard, Two-way Audio

CLOSER
LEARNING ACTIVITY
OPENER
SOFT OPENER
ENERGIZER
REVISITER

GROUP WORK

Purpose
Apply Material, Brainstorm, Combining, Establish a Learning Community, Familiarizing, Innovate New Ideas, Recall Background Knowledge, Recall Information—Existing Schemas, Revisit, Teach New Material

Setup
- Create a list of participants who will be in a group together. This can also be identified in the moment if participant numbers are unclear.
- Create a slide that includes the following:
    o Title: "Creative Crew" or "Tactical Tribe"
    o "Share the following with each other:
        - Who you are
        - One tip you have for [insert content being covered]
        - What you are looking forward to during this session"
    o "Team moderator is the person with the longest first name."
- Insert the slides wherever this content falls in the presentation.

Trainer Process

- Split learners into groups of two to four people in each breakout room.
- Share that they will be going into breakout rooms in a moment. The tools are the same as in the main room and they will see the same slide as a reminder of what to do.
- Groups will have 5 minutes to answer the questions.
- Have groups "discuss" and, using the webinar platform tools (different colors, drawing tools, text, etc.), write these on their whiteboards.
- After the time is up, everyone will be back in the main room. Let these groups know they will be connecting with their "crew" throughout the session.
- Share how learners can get your attention for questions while in their rooms.
- Once learners are in their breakouts, move from room to room, clarifying as needed.
- Have all groups come back together and have the team's moderators share what their group is looking forward to.

Producer Process

- Create breakout rooms.
- Post pre-made slide in each breakout room with instructions.
- Put up a timer for 5 minutes and have it count down.
- Answer any questions that come through via text chat.
- Check in on breakout rooms and answer any questions.
- After time is up, post breakout room whiteboards in the main room for viewing or application share the whiteboards.

Variations

- With small groups, do this in the main room as one large group.
- Use this group or crew to brainstorm any topic or idea. Continually break back into the same group to problem solve or generate ideas on how to adapt, adopt or apply the material being taught.
- If first-time learners have not been in a breakout room before, don't have participants worry about tools—just have them share their ideas out loud.

WEBINAR LENGTH: Any
ACTIVITY LENGTH: 1-5 minutes
INSTRUCTOR SKILL LEVEL: Novice
PARTICIPANT SKILL LEVEL: Novice
SUPPLIES: Slide
TOOLS: Polling

CLOSER
LEARNING ACTIVITY
OPENER
SOFT OPENER
ENERGIZER
REVISITER

HEART SMART

Purpose
Establishing a Learning Community, Refocus Learner

Setup
- Create a slide that includes the following:
  o Title: Heart Smart
  o "Raise your online hand and stand up if the listed idea is healthy."
  o "Put down your online hand if the listed idea is unhealthy."
- Create slide(s) that include the following ideas (do not include the sit/stand after the statement on the slide; they are for facilitator reference only). List of possible ideas:
  o Riding a bike — stand
  o Eating four pepperoni pizzas — sit
  o Walking your dog — stand
  o Smoking cigarettes — sit
  o Dancing with your friends — stand
  o Skating — stand
  o Playing PlayStation — sit
  o Eating fast food — sit
  o Taking the stairs — stand
  o Taking the elevator — sit

- Insert the slide anywhere throughout the presentation for fun as an energizer.

Trainer Process
- Put up the "Heart Smart" direction slide when learners are starting to fade.
- Review the instructions on the slide.
  - Raise your online hand and stand up if the listed idea is healthy.
  - Put down your online hand if the listed idea is unhealthy.
- Share that a slide will be posted with a habit that strengthens or weakens the heart.
- If the habit strengthens the heart, participants should respond by standing up and raising their online hand. Demonstrate by raising your hand.
- If the habit weakens the heart, participants should respond by sitting down in their chair and lowering or keeping their hand down.
- Encourage participation by demonstrating the movements on a webcam.
- After all listed ideas are done, ask participants to text chat how they are feeling now compared to before they took their heart smart break.

Producer Process
- Put on your webcam and participate.
- Post ideas on whiteboard to get learners thinking (variation only).
- Put up timer for 30-45 seconds (variation only).

Variations
- Have learners stand and text chat when they did the last "Heart Smart" ideas.
- In need of a quick unplanned energizer? Put up a blank whiteboard and have learners post, one at a time, healthy and unhealthy ideas. It is quick and easy to throw in at any time.
- Do as a timed activity and get through as many as possible in the allotted time.
- Have participants text chat, instead of whiteboard, healthy habits they can think of.

WEBINAR LENGTH: Any
ACTIVITY LENGTH: 20-30 minutes
INSTRUCTOR SKILL LEVEL: Intermediate
PARTICIPANT SKILL LEVEL: Intermediate
SUPPLIES: Slide
TOOLS: Breakout Rooms, Group Whiteboard, Two-way Audio

CLOSER
LEARNING ACTIVITY
OPENER
SOFT OPENER
ENERGIZER
REVISITER

I OBJECT

I Object!

Insert Objection #1
Insert Objection #2
Insert Objection #3
Insert Objection #4

Team Leader: Person with the least years with the organization.

Purpose

Apply Material, Brainstorm, Combining, Establish a Learning Community, Familiarizing, Innovate New Ideas, Recall Background Knowledge, Recall Information—Existing Schemas, Revisit, Teach New Material

Setup

- Create a list of participants who will be in a group together. This can also be identified in the moment if participant numbers are unclear.
- Create a slide that includes the following:
  o Title: I Object!
  o Three to four different objections you have heard about the content, product, skill, and the list goes on.
  o "Team moderator is the person with the least number of years with the organization."
- Create a separate slide for each of the objections to be placed in breakout rooms with the "I Object" instructions slide.
- Insert the slides wherever this content falls in the presentation.

Trainer Process

- Split learners into breakout rooms with two to four people in each.
- Each group is given a turn to select an objection from the list to work on in their breakout room.
- Each objection can be selected only once.
- Groups will have 3-7 minutes (depending on knowledge level and time needed) to use prior knowledge and new learning to overcome their objection.
- Have groups "discuss" and, using the webinar platform tools (different colors, drawing tools, text, etc.), write these on their whiteboards.
- For example, participants can respond to an objection by stating a fact or feature about the product, and relating it, as a benefit, to the client's known needs.
- After the time is up, everyone will be back in the main room to share their objection and how they overcame it.
- Share how learners can ask you questions while in their rooms.
- Once learners are in their breakout rooms, move from room to room clarifying as needed.
- Have all groups come back together. The team's moderators will share their whiteboard with the group. Any ideas that are duplicated do not need to be covered again.

Producer Process

- Create breakout rooms.
- Post pre-made slide with an objection in each breakout room with instructions.
- Put up a timer for 3-7 minutes and have it count down.
- Answer any questions that come through via text chat.
- Check in on breakout rooms and answer any questions.
- After time is up, post breakout room whiteboards in the main room for viewing or application share the whiteboards.

Variations

- With small groups, do this in the main room together.
- Have breakout room groups come up with their own objection that another group will try to overcome.

WEBINAR LENGTH: Any
ACTIVITY LENGTH: 5-10 minutes
INSTRUCTOR SKILL LEVEL: Novice
PARTICIPANT SKILL LEVEL: Novice
SUPPLIES: Slide
TOOLS: Group Whiteboard

CLOSER
LEARNING ACTIVITY
OPENER
SOFT OPENER
ENERGIZER
REVISITER

IDENTIFICATION SHUFFLE

Purpose
Familiarizing, Introduce New Concept, Preview Material, Recall Background Knowledge, Recall Information—Existing Schemas, Revisit, Teach New Material

Setup
- Create an "Identification Shuffle" slide that includes the following:
   o   Title: Identification Shuffle
   o   Investigative image inserted as a background
   o   Place eight to 10 correct process steps or concepts in a theory and eight to 10 incorrect process steps or concepts in a theory. Have them mixed together.
- Insert the slide into the presentation in the beginning as an opener, partway through the webinar if used as a revisiter or, if used as a closer, before a break or at the very end of the session. This can also be used at any point to transition content to a new topic or as a learning activity to solidify steps in a process.
- Create a handout page that lists all the steps in the correct sequence.

Trainer Process

- Have learners close their workbooks for the next activity.
- Put up the "Identification Shuffle" slide.
- Have learners highlight an item in red that is not part of the process or highlight in green an item that is part of the process. Learners will take turns highlighting one item.
- If a participant doesn't know, they can then opt to type a number next to one of the items already highlighted to identify what step is first, second, third and so on in the process. If introducing a new topic, guessing is to be expected.
- Rotate around the group until all items are highlighted and numbered in the correct order.
- After each item is either removed or moved into sequence, talk about why it fits there and its importance to the process.
- After all items are done, discuss which items were correctly or incorrectly moved and spend some time on the errors and how to recall important steps or concepts.
- Refer learners to the page in their workbooks that has the items in the correct sequence.

Producer Process

- Put up a timer for 1-3 minutes and have it count down or up (variation only).

Variations

- If the platform being used allows for animation, insert hyperlinks that move the elements to a correct or incorrect side of the page so all that participants have to do is click on the item.
- If your platform allows, click and drag the item to the correct side of the slide or to arrange it in the right sequence. Remove the item if it is not part of the sequence.
- To add to the fun, put on a timer or stopwatch to see how long it takes. You can also use a countdown timer and see how far they have gotten when time is up. The pieces that are out of order can then be discussed further.

WEBINAR LENGTH: Any
ACTIVITY LENGTH: 5-10 minutes
INSTRUCTOR SKILL LEVEL: Intermediate
PARTICIPANT SKILL LEVEL: Intermediate
SUPPLIES: Pre-made Interactive Game, Hyperlink to Activity
TOOLS: Group Text Chat, Polling

CLOSER
LEARNING ACTIVITY
OPENER
SOFT OPENER
ENERGIZER
REVISITER

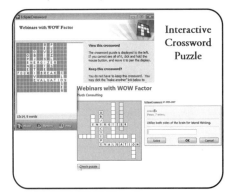

INTERACTIVE CROSSWORD PUZZLE

Purpose
Familiarizing, Introduce New Concept, Preview Material, Recall Background Knowledge, Refocus Learner, Revisit

Setup
- Create a list of words that learners should become aware of or know by the end of a session. For each word, create a clue.
- Ensure the selected crossword product can be played online. One I recommend for Microsoft users is EclipseCrossword.com. It has several different printing options. For interaction, the site can save your crossword as a web page that won't require new software for users to download.
- Go through the tutorial if you want to be guided through the process.
- Once created, copy and paste the link into the leader's guide for quick reference.
- Take a screenshot of the game. Use this as your "Interactive Crossword Puzzle" slide and insert it into the slide deck at the appropriate point.
- Create a "Word List" slide with a list of all the words used in the crossword puzzle.

- Insert both slides, one after the other, in the beginning of the presentation if used as an opener for term recognition, at the end as the closer to reinforce concepts, or anywhere throughout to be used as an energizer, revisiter or learning activity.

Trainer Process

- Put up the "Interactive Crossword" slide.
- Share with learners that they will have 3 minutes (or longer or shorter depending on the length of word search) to complete the crossword.
- Have learners click on the hyperlink in the text chat area (or copy and paste the link into a web browser if clicking doesn't work) and proceed to find the words.
- Put up the "Word List" slide.
- After the timer runs out, ask learners to raise their hand or select an emoticon to show that they are back in the room.
- See how learners did and where they struggled.
- Briefly go through and see what terms participants are unfamiliar with and provide explanations.

Producer Process

- Make sure the link is working just before the session begins.
- Type the link into the text chat area for learners.
- Watch the text chat area for any questions.

Variations

- Application share a web browser, and show learners what the crossword puzzle looks like while explaining how to do it. Model selecting a link.
- Give the link out in a welcome letter as a pre-session assignment.
- Use as a follow-up exercise for learners to recall information after the class.
- Save the crossword as a PDF or use the print options for inside the learner workbook.

Webinars with WOW Factor

WEBINAR LENGTH: Any
ACTIVITY LENGTH: 5-10 minutes
INSTRUCTOR SKILL LEVEL: Intermediate
PARTICIPANT SKILL LEVEL: Intermediate
SUPPLIES: Pre-made Interactive Game, Hyperlink to Activity
TOOLS: Group Text Chat, Polling

CLOSER
LEARNING ACTIVITY
OPENER
SOFT OPENER
ENERGIZER
REVISITER

INTERACTIVE WORD SEARCH

Purpose
Familiarizing, Introduce New Concept, Preview Material, Recall Background Knowledge, Refocus Learner, Revisit

Setup
- Create a word search, a grid of letters learners search through to find "hidden terms" associated with session content. Determine how hard you want to make the puzzle. The more ways a word can be found—vertically, horizontally, diagonally, backward and forward—the more difficult the puzzle.
- Ensure the word search product you use can be played online. One free online tool that can be used so all your learners can digitally "play" can be found on the Teacher's Direct website at http://bit.ly/wordfind. URL is case sensitive.
    o   Title the word search, then select any subject, then choose the size and type of search you wish to create. Select "15x15" for grid size, "interactive word search" for the word search type, and "lower case" for the text case. Then input the terms. Once completed, paste the link provided in your webinar so that learners can paste it in their browsers and quickly get to the word search.

- Take a screenshot of the game and use as your "Interactive Word Search" slide. Insert into the slide deck early in your presentation to help learners recognize terms, or place it later to reinforce terminology.
- Create a "Word List" slide with a list of all the words used in the word search.
- Insert both slides together at the beginning of the presentation if used as an opener, at the end as the closer or anywhere throughout to be used as an energizer, revisiter or learning activity.

Trainer Process

- Put up the "Interactive Word Search" slide.
- Share with learners that they will have 3 minutes (longer or shorter depending on length of word search) to complete the word search.
- As they find words they are unfamiliar with, they should jot them down to explore once they are back in the webinar.
- Have learners click on the hyperlink in the text chat area (or copy and paste the link into a web browser) and find the words.
- Put up the "Word List" slide.
- After the timer runs out, ask learners to raise their hand or select an emoticon to show that they are back in the room.
- Briefly go through and see what terms participants are unfamiliar with and provide an explanation.

Producer Process

- Make sure the link is working just before the session begins.
- Type the link into the text chat area for learners.
- Watch the text chat area for any questions.

Variations

- Application share a web browser and show learners what the interactive word search looks like while explaining how to do it. Model selecting a link.
- Give the link in a welcome letter as a pre-session assignment.
- Use as a follow-up exercise for learners to recall information after the class.
- Save the word search as a PDF or print it for inside the learner workbook.

WEBINAR LENGTH: Any
ACTIVITY LENGTH: 5 minutes
INSTRUCTOR SKILL LEVEL: Novice
PARTICIPANT SKILL LEVEL: Novice
SUPPLIES: Slide
TOOLS: Group Whiteboard

CLOSER
LEARNING ACTIVITY
OPENER
SOFT OPENER
ENERGIZER
REVISITER

LITERARY ASSUMPTIONS

Purpose
Brainstorm, Establish a Learning Community, Familiarizing, Introduce New Concept, Recall Background Knowledge, Recall Information—Existing Schemas, Refocus Learner, Teach New Material

Setup
- Create a slide that includes the following (these can be split into individual slides):
    o Title: Literary Assumptions
    o ~~CHANGE IS A CORE CONCEPT~~
    o ~~CHUNK CONCEPTS INTO SMALL PARTS~~
    o "Directions: Decipher the hidden message just from the partial letters you see."
- Create a second slide that includes the answer. Samples:
    o "CHANGE IS A CORE CONCEPT"
    o "CHUNK CONTENT INTO SMALL PARTS"
- Insert the slide into the beginning of the presentation if it is to be used as a soft opener. Then put up the slide prior to the webinar to help acclimate learners to the platform tools. If this is to be used as an opener, insert the slide at the start of the session. To use this as an energizer, insert the slide anywhere.

Trainer Process

- Put up the "Literary Assumptions" slide.
- Ask learners to decipher the hidden message just from the partial letters they see and whiteboard their guesses.
- After 90 seconds, continue to the next content piece if this is used as an energizer. If this is used as an opener, ask participants to whiteboard what insights can be taken away from this exercise.
    - o Look for: sometimes when doing things too quickly, assumptions are made from past experience; when we are experts, we take what we know for granted; common knowledge can get in the way of seeing things clearly.

Producer Process

- Welcome participants as they enter the virtual room via text chat.
- Whiteboard an idea or two to spur thoughts.
- Turn on the timer for 30-60 seconds (variation only).

Variations

- Create a phrase that directly relates to the content being taught.
- Have a dialogue with learners about assumptions via two-way audio. Call on participants one at a time.
- Have learners work individually at first to come up with words and then, after 30-60 seconds, have them work together. Debrief with questions like: What helped you to be successful? What does success look like? What insights can we take away from this exercise and apply back at work?
- Tie the puzzle to the content whenever possible.
- Use the puzzle to transition to a new topic.

WEBINAR LENGTH: Any
ACTIVITY LENGTH: 5 minutes
INSTRUCTOR SKILL LEVEL: Novice
PARTICIPANT SKILL LEVEL: Novice
SUPPLIES: Slide
TOOLS: Group Whiteboard, Group Text Chat

CLOSER
LEARNING ACTIVITY
OPENER
SOFT OPENER
ENERGIZER
REVISITER

Map It – Where are we?

MAP IT

Purpose
Brainstorm, Establish a Learning Community

Setup
- Create a slide that includes the following (these can be split into individual slides):
  o Title: Where Are We?
  o Large image of the United States (or world map or state map)
  o Directions: Using a pointer or highlighter, mark the spot where you are right now.
- Insert the slide into the beginning of the presentation if it is to be used as a soft opener. Then put up the slide prior to the webinar to help acclimate learners to the platform tools. If this is to be used as an opener, insert the slide at the start of the session. To use this as an energizer, insert the slide anywhere.

Trainer Process

- Put up the "Where Are We?" slide.
- Ask learners to use their tools and point or highlight the spot where they are located. Then have learners text chat the exact location and what the weather is like.
- Model highlighting on the whiteboard and text chat what the weather is like.
- Act as an announcer and read off where people are from.

Producer Process

- Welcome participants as they enter the virtual room via text chat.
- Highlight on whiteboard where you are at and text chat the weather there.

Variations

- If using two-way audio, have participants, one at a time, share a little about their climate or what they are looking forward to.
- Ask learners questions or trivia about their state.
- After highlighting where they are, have learners highlight where they are dreaming of going or where they wish they were on the map. Text chat the exact location and why.

WEBINAR LENGTH: > 60 minutes
ACTIVITY LENGTH: 10-15 minutes
INSTRUCTOR SKILL LEVEL: Intermediate
PARTICIPANT SKILL LEVEL: Intermediate
SUPPLIES: Slide
TOOLS: Breakout Rooms, Group Whiteboard, Two-way Audio

CLOSER
LEARNING ACTIVITY
OPENER
SOFT OPENER
ENERGIZER
REVISITER

MASTERMIND MIX

Purpose
Brainstorm, Establish a Learning Community, Familiarizing, Introduce New Concept, Recall Background Knowledge, Recall Information—Existing Schemas, Refocus Learner

Setup
- Determine the number of participants and what breakout rooms will be named.
- Create a slide that includes the following:
    o   Title: Mastermind Mix
    o   The image in the background should be of two minds meeting
    o   "Each member introduce yourself"
    o   "Share one fact, concept or idea you already know about today's webinar or topic"
- Insert the slide into the presentation in the beginning as an opener or anywhere throughout the session as an energizer.

Trainer Process

- Put up the "Mastermind Mix" slide.
- Share that there are participants in this webinar who are going to really take their level of understanding with this topic to a new level. There are several who already know something about the webinar topic, whether it be a piece of data, terminology or something about using webinars.
- Have learners take a look at the list of names of those in the session.
- Share that it is an honor to be on this webinar with everyone and that they will find masters all throughout our list.
- Share that learners will be in breakout rooms in a moment. They will have 3 minutes to introduce themselves, and share one fact, concept or idea about the session topic they already know. This will then become their Mastermind group for the session. From time to time, they will have a "meeting of the minds" and be breaking out with them.
- Ask if there are questions about the directions.
- Split participants into breakout rooms with three to five participants in each.
- Send groups into their assigned breakout rooms for 3 minutes.
- Return teams to the main room.

Producer Process

- Create breakout rooms.
- Post the "Mastermind Mix" slide in each breakout room.
- Send learners into their breakout rooms.
- Put up a timer for 3 minutes and have it count down.
- Check in on breakout rooms and answer any questions.

Variations

- If you have a small group, stay in the main room together.
- Have learners create a whiteboard that represents their mastermind team and what they shared with each other.

WEBINAR LENGTH: > 90 minutes
ACTIVITY LENGTH: 6-13 minutes
INSTRUCTOR SKILL LEVEL: Novice
PARTICIPANT SKILL LEVEL: Novice
SUPPLIES: Slide
TOOLS: Whiteboard

CLOSER
LEARNING ACTIVITY
OPENER
SOFT OPENER
ENERGIZER
REVISITER

ONE AND DONE BREAK (AKA THE ONE-FUNCTION BREAK)

Purpose
Refocus Learner

Setup

- Determine the length of the break. The longer the webinar, the longer the break. Break times that work well:
  o   2-hour session = 6- to 8-minute break at the 60-minute mark
  o   2 ½-hour session = 9- to 10-minute break between 75-90 minutes
  o   3-hour session = 11- to 15-minute break at the 90-minute mark OR two shorter breaks at the 1-and 2-hour marks. Depending on the content, it may be better to provide two 6-minute breaks to help with the flow of content. If concerned about participants not arriving back on time from shorter breaks, opt for one longer break.
- Create a slide and include the following:
  o   Title: One and Done Break
  o   The amount of time the break will be
- Insert the slide into the session at the 60-, 75- or 90-minute mark.

Trainer Process

- Explain that the group will be taking a "One and Done" break in a moment.
- Put up the "One and Done" slide.
- Describe the break: You have time to smoke or make a phone call, use the restroom, check an email or text chat us a question, but not time for all.
- Don't fret about losing people. If your content is interactive and engaging, they'll be back.

Producer Process

- Put up a timer and have it count down.
- Answer any questions that come through via text chat.
- Create breakout rooms and distribute participants (variation only).
- Check in on breakout rooms and help answer questions (variation only).

Variations

- Create assignments for each person to accomplish while on break. This would be considered a "working break" where there is enough time to accomplish the task and still have time left over for a one and done break.
- Extend the break time and incorporate a small group discussion in breakout rooms with teach-back points they are responsible for sharing with the large group.

WEBINAR LENGTH: Any
ACTIVITY LENGTH: 2-5 minutes
INSTRUCTOR SKILL LEVEL: Novice
PARTICIPANT SKILL LEVEL: Novice
SUPPLIES: Slide
TOOLS: Polling, Two-way Audio

CLOSER
LEARNING ACTIVITY
OPENER
SOFT OPENER
ENERGIZER
REVISITER

OOHHRAH CHEER

Purpose
Apply Material, Combining, Familiarizing, Recall Background Knowledge, Recall Information—Existing Schemas, Revisit

Setup
- Create the session slide deck
- Within the deck, insert errors
  - Errors could be anything from changing the name of a product, giving an incorrect data piece (later in the presentation) to spelling or grammatical errors.
  - Errors later in the deck should be about content previously learned to be used as a revisit technique.
- Insert slides wherever they would fall in the content flow. Purposely insert errors throughout at good revisit points.

Trainer Process

- At the beginning of the session, let learners know that errors have been "planted" on slides and that there are fabulous semi-valuable prizes for those who catch the errors.
- Whenever a participant catches an error, they may raise their virtual hand, be called on, turn on their microphone and cheer "OOHHRAH."
- They will then share what the error was and how it should be corrected.
- If learners miss a content error, pause and ask, "What is wrong with this slide?"
- Wait and see if they can figure it out.

Producer Process

- Keep track of error slides and prompt the facilitator if one is missed.
- Keep track of learners who raise their hand and shout OOOHHRAH.
- Send out a prize to the winning participant.

Variations

- At the end of the session, ask learners to whiteboard or chat about this question: "What does finding errors in this session have to do with our topic today?" Look for things that relate to the session. For example: stopping to correct errors right away saves time and money.
- Instead of shouting OOHHRAH, have learners highlight anything they find wrong as an error along the way.

WEBINAR LENGTH: Any
ACTIVITY LENGTH: 1-5 minutes
INSTRUCTOR SKILL LEVEL: Novice
PARTICIPANT SKILL LEVEL: Novice
SUPPLIES: Slide, UNO cards optional
TOOLS: Whiteboard

CLOSER
LEARNING ACTIVITY
OPENER
SOFT OPENER
ENERGIZER
REVISITER

PASS IT ON— UNO™ STYLE

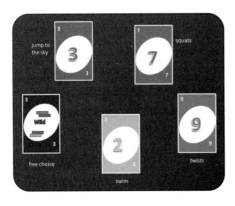

Purpose
Establishing a Learning Community, Refocus Learner

Setup
- Create an "UNO" slide that includes the following:
    o Images of UNO-style cards. At least one of each color card should be represented. Include a wild card.
- Create a second slide that includes the following:
    o Blue: jump to the sky
    o Red: squats
    o Yellow: twist
    o Green: swim
    o Wild: free choice
- Insert the slide anywhere in the deck for fun as an energizer.

Trainer Process
- Put up the "UNO" slide when learners are starting to fade.
- Have a participant volunteer and select an UNO card from the screen and circle it.
- Once circled, share that this is the activity they get to do for 30 seconds to get the blood moving.
- If a wild card is selected, it is free choice for the activity.
- Turn on your webcam to demonstrate the 30-second activity.
- After the timer is done, ask participants to text chat how they are feeling now compared to before they took a "swim."

Producer Process
- Put up the timer for 30 seconds.

Variations
- Instead of 30 seconds, base it on the number selected. The number selected equals the number of times the activity is done. Example: If a red 7 is selected, participants would do seven squats.
- Create a slide with enough UNO cards so that each person will have one. Each participant circles a card on the whiteboard and types their name above or below the card. After they have completed the activity associated with their card, they pass their card to another participant by drawing a line to another card.
- If using a webcam, hold up a deck of UNO cards and have a learner tell you when to stop. The card stopped on is the card selected. Continue with the same exercise rules.

WEBINAR LENGTH: Any
ACTIVITY LENGTH: 5 minutes
INSTRUCTOR SKILL LEVEL: Novice
PARTICIPANT SKILL LEVEL: Novice
SUPPLIES: Slide
TOOLS: Group Text Chat

CLOSER
LEARNING ACTIVITY
OPENER
SOFT OPENER
ENERGIZER
REVISITER

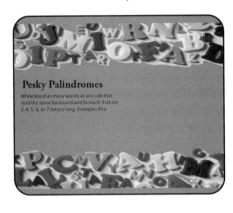

PESKY PALINDROMES

Purpose
Establish a Learning Community, Introduce New Concept, Refocus Learner

Setup
- Create a slide that includes the following (these can be split into individual slides):
  o Title: Pesky Palindromes
  o Image in the background of a lot of scattered letters.
  o "Whiteboard as many words as you can that read the same backward and forward that are 3, 4, 5, 6 or 7 letters long. Example: aha"
- Create a second slide that includes some answers (optional):
  o 3 letters—aha, bib, dad, did, hah, mom, bob, tot, wow
  o 4 letters—noon, peep, poop, ma'am, sees, toot
  o 5 letters—kayak, level, madam, stats, radar, refer, rotor, sexes
  o 6 letters—redder, denned
  o 7 letters—racecar, repaper, reviver, rotator, deified, a Toyota

- Insert the slide into the beginning of the presentation if it is to be used as a soft opener. Then put up the slide prior to the webinar to help acclimate learners to the platform tools. If this is to be used as an opener, insert the slide at the start of the session. To use this as an energizer, insert the slide anywhere.

Trainer Process

- Put up the "Pesky Palindromes" slide.
- Ask learners to text chat their ideas for 60 seconds.
- After time is up, move on to the next slide.
- Discuss connections between palindromes and what is being learned or will be learned. Have learners text chat their ideas. Read them out loud as they come up.
    o   Look for: look at information from multiple angles and make sure we get the same answer; the longer the process, the more difficult to ensure it works both ways.
- No matter the length of the palindrome, the exercise can be used as a quick way to energize a group and get brain cells firing again.

Producer Process

- Welcome participants as they enter the virtual room via text chat.

Variations

- Create a list of just the first and last letter of the palindrome and see how many get filled in. Example: A_A, B_B, K _ _ K, R _ _ _ R and so on. Time it for 30 seconds for a quick energizer.
- Brainstorm only three-letter words for quicker reaction and response. For more advanced critical thinkers, limit responses to five-letters or longer.
- Tie the word puzzle to the content whenever possible. Use the word puzzle to transition to a new topic.

WEBINAR LENGTH: Any
ACTIVITY LENGTH: 1-5 minutes
INSTRUCTOR SKILL LEVEL: Novice
PARTICIPANT SKILL LEVEL: Novice
SUPPLIES: Slide
TOOLS: Polling

CLOSER
LEARNING ACTIVITY
OPENER
SOFT OPENER
ENERGIZER
REVISITER

POP QUIZ
POP PUZZLE

Purpose
Apply Material, Introduce New Concept, Preview Material, Recall Background Knowledge, Recall Information—Existing Schemas, Refocus Learner, Revisit, Teach New Material

Setup
- Become familiar with polling options on the platform you will be using.
- Create pre-made "Pop Quiz" question slide(s) and include a small screenshot of where the polling icons are located.
- Write up to three questions on each slide that relate to content that was or will be covered during the session.
   o   Number the questions.
   o   Create as many question slides as desired.
   o   Create a Pop Quiz answer slide(s). Put all questions and their answers on the slide(s). Number each answer.
- Quiz questions on each slide should all be the same type: Yes/No, True/False, A-E etc.
- Insert the "Pop Quiz" slides as the first slide if used as an opener to get a pulse on where learners are at with the content.

- Insert throughout for revisiting or energizing and at the end as the last slide if closing out the session with a "Pop Quiz."
- Insert the "Pop Quiz" answer slide(s) after each "Pop Quiz" slide or after the final "Pop Quiz."

Trainer Process

- Put up the first "Pop Quiz" slide.
- Explain that throughout the webinar there will be "Pop Quiz" slides.
- When these slides "pop up," each person will use their polling tools to answer the questions.
- After everyone has answered, show the learner results, and then the correct answer can be defined. If used as an opener, follow each slide up with teaching the content from the slide questions. If the platform doesn't allow for results to be shown, have learners keep track of their answers and correct themselves when the answer slide is revealed.

PRODUCER PROCESS

- Prior to the questions going up on the whiteboard, be sure to change polling from a pacing feature to a yes/no feature or true/false question if the correct polling features are not standard on the platform.

VARIATIONS

- The term "quiz" may have negative connotations. To make it more fun and light, use the word "puzzle" instead.
- If you need a quick engager and haven't had a chance to prepare a slide, add a whiteboard and insert a question in the moment.
- Have a competitive crowd? Grade the quizzes and have learners keep track of their own score. Award more points for harder questions. Add the point value to each slide.
- Pop quizzes do not need to be graded; however, they give the facilitator a pulse as to what may need reemphasizing.
- If the platform being used doesn't have polling options, create the questions and answers on a whiteboard and have participants highlight or mark the answer they think is correct.

WEBINAR LENGTH: Any
ACTIVITY LENGTH: 1-5 minutes
INSTRUCTOR SKILL LEVEL: Novice
PARTICIPANT SKILL LEVEL: Novice
SUPPLIES: Slide
TOOLS: Group Text Chat, Polling

CLOSER
LEARNING ACTIVITY
OPENER
SOFT OPENER
ENERGIZER
REVISITER

POP UPS

Purpose
Apply Material, Introduce New Concept, Preview Material, Recall Background Knowledge, Recall Information—Existing Schemas, Refocus Learner, Revisit, Teach New Material

Setup
- Create a "Pop Up" rules slide with the following rules:
    o 1st person to raise hand=answer question
    o 2nd person to raise hand=select exercise
    o Everyone=pop up and do exercise while question is being answered [modify these rules as needed].
- Create pre-made question slide(s) and include a small screenshot of where the "raise hand" icon is located.
    o Write one question on the slide about content covered.
    o Across the bottom of the slide, list out five different types of exercises. Examples: Toe Touch, Twists, Jumping Jacks
    o Create as many question slides as needed.
- Become familiar with signals on the platform you will be using.
- Insert the "Pop Up" rules slide toward the beginning of the presentation but after the webinar opener and session agenda.

- Insert the slide(s) into the presentation at any point as an energizer and revisit technique. Increase the number of "Pop Up" slides as presentations get longer.

Trainer Process

- Put up the "Pop Up" rules slide.
- Explain that throughout the webinar there will be "Pop Up" slides that look like this. Put up an example of a "Pop Up" question slide.
- When these slides "pop up," the first person to raise their hand and share the answer receives a point.
- Points can accumulate during single or multiple sessions. Pop ups can also be random facts about the company or product.
- The second person to raise their hand selects one of the exercises listed on the bottom of the "Pop Up" question slide. All other learners then "Pop Up" and do the exercise continuously while the first person answers the question.
- If the question is answered incorrectly, the question goes to the second person who raises their hand. If it is still answered incorrectly, the instructor reveals the answer to the group.
- Turn on your webcam to demonstrate standing up and then model the selected exercise.

Producer Process

- Before the questions go on the whiteboard, make sure the polling has the correct features (e.g., from pacing to yes/no) if the polling features are not standard on the platform.

Variations

- If you need a quick engager and haven't had a chance to prepare a slide, just add a whiteboard and insert a question in the moment.
- Have a competitive crowd? Late in the day put up a timer for 2-5 minutes and have learners answer as many "Pop Up" questions as possible to earn last minute points.
- Double the pop up point value in the last portion of the webinar.
- If a "raise hand" signal button isn't available on your platform, try using a different signal button. This could be a smiley face or learners could clap.

Webinars with WOW Factor

WEBINAR LENGTH: Any
ACTIVITY LENGTH: 5-15 minutes
INSTRUCTOR SKILL LEVEL: Novice
PARTICIPANT SKILL LEVEL: Novice
SUPPLIES: Slide
TOOLS: Whiteboard and Drawing/Writing Tools – Optional Text Chat, Breakout Rooms

CLOSER
LEARNING ACTIVITY
OPENER
SOFT OPENER
ENERGIZER
REVISITER

Q IT UP

Purpose
Brainstorm, Establish a Learning Community, Introduce New Concept, Recall Background Knowledge, Revisit

Setup
- Create a handout titled "Questions" for learners to compile questions during the webinar.
- Create a slide that includes the following:
    o Title: Q It Up
    o Image of a large "?"
- Insert the slide into the presentation at the beginning of a second webinar as an opener, anywhere throughout to revisit or energize, before a break or at the very end of the session as a closing exercise.

Trainer Process
- Have learners turn to their "Questions" page.
- Put up the "Q It Up" slide.
- Share that the group will have 60 seconds to review their questions and cross off questions that have been answered. Then they may post as many questions as they are able on the whiteboard or in the text chat in the time allotted.

- When working with the same learners over the course of several webinars, there may be "parking lot" questions that need to be answered, also.
- Answer posted questions from the whiteboard and parking lot.
- If used as a closer, each participant can write a question on the whiteboard from content that was already covered. In some cases they may already know the answer; in others, they may have missed something and need the information. After questions are up, each participant text chats (or writes on the whiteboard) the answer to a question they did not write. These questions can then be used in a subsequent webinar as quiz questions or for another exercise.
- If used as a revisit or opener technique, have learners write their questions in the first webinar and have each question posted in the second webinar. Each group will take a question and have 2-4 minutes in their breakout rooms to come up with an answer. Alternately, pre-select questions at random and post in their breakout rooms. Learners will write the answer to their question(s) on the whiteboard. Bring everyone back into the main room and go from one question to the next with their posted answers.

Producer Process
- Put up a timer for 60 seconds.
- Answer/post any questions that come through via text chat.
- Copy whiteboard questions for future use.
- Put up a timer for 5 minutes (variation only).

Variations
- Use pre-made content questions and have learners post their answers on the whiteboard. Or post the answer and have learners whiteboard the question.
- To ensure the question-and-answer session doesn't take too long, use a countdown timer and post 5 minutes.
- Have learners post only questions for which they do not have an answer.

WEBINAR LENGTH: Any
ACTIVITY LENGTH: 1-5 minutes
INSTRUCTOR SKILL LEVEL: Novice
PARTICIPANT SKILL LEVEL: Novice
SUPPLIES: Slide
TOOLS: Group Whiteboard

CLOSER
LEARNING ACTIVITY
OPENER
SOFT OPENER
ENERGIZER
REVISITER

QUICK QUESTIONS

Purpose
Apply Material, Recall Background Knowledge, Refocus Learner, Revisit

Setup
- Create a list of questions pertaining to the content and have it written down in the leader's guide.
- Create a list of acceptable answers to those questions.
- Create a slide(s) that has a list of all the questions and answers (Q&A).

Trainer Process

- At any time in the session, insert a clean whiteboard slide and type a question to interject some variety and interest.
- Announce that learners will only have a set amount of time (30 seconds) to jot down their answer on note paper.
- Do this several times throughout the webinar.
- At the end of the session, take those same questions and have people share their answers at random.
- Thank the learners for sharing.
- Post the "Q&A" slide for all to see acceptable answers.

Producer Process

- Put up a timer for 30 seconds.
- Capture learner questions (variation only).

Variations

- Make it competitive and the person with the most correct answers wins a small prize.
- Have learners volunteer to post a question in the moment.

WEBINAR LENGTH: Any
ACTIVITY LENGTH: 5-20 minutes
INSTRUCTOR SKILL LEVEL: Intermediate
PARTICIPANT SKILL LEVEL: Novice
SUPPLIES: Slide
TOOLS: Application Share, Two-way Audio

CLOSER
LEARNING ACTIVITY
OPENER
SOFT OPENER
ENERGIZER
REVISITER

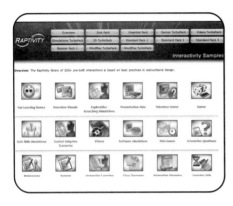

RAPTIVITY™

Purpose
Apply Material, Brainstorm, Combining, Establish a Learning Community, Familiarizing, Innovate New Ideas, Introduce New Concept, Preview Material, Recall Background Knowledge, Recall Information—Existing Schemas, Refocus Learner, Revisit, Teach New Material

Setup
- Purchase Raptivity software or download a free trial license at Raptivity.com.
- Select an interactive game that suits the content. More than 225 interactive options are available, ranging from videos to simulations to matching games. All are colorful and all can be housed online for learners to do on their own.
- Create and test the game.
- Create a slide that includes the following:
    o Directions on how the game works. This will vary based on the exercise selected by the facilitator.

Trainer Process

- Launch the Raptivity game.
- Start the game and ask participants to raise their hand if they think they know the answer.
- Continue getting answers to game questions until the exercise is done.
- Stop application sharing and have participants text chat learnings from the exercise. Continue with a lecturette on the topics or content covered.

Producer Process

- Monitor text chat and respond to questions.

Variations

- For more experienced users, turn over control to a participant and have them click through the game and get answers from the group.
- Have learners go through the game on their own and then application share the game and talk through the different concepts and elements.
- Intersperse the game throughout the session and do a few questions or elements at a time.

WEBINAR LENGTH: Any
ACTIVITY LENGTH: 5 minutes
INSTRUCTOR SKILL LEVEL: Novice
PARTICIPANT SKILL LEVEL: Novice
SUPPLIES: Slide
TOOLS: Group Text Chat

CLOSER
LEARNING ACTIVITY
OPENER
SOFT OPENER
ENERGIZER
REVISITER

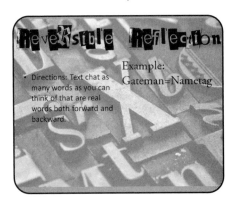

REVERSIBLE REFLECTION

Purpose
Establish a Learning Community, Introduce New Concept, Refocus Learner

Setup
- Create a slide that includes the following (these can be split into individual slides):
    o   Title: Reversible Reflection
    o   Image in the background of a lot of random words scattered around as a watermark.
- Directions: Text chat as many words as you can that are real words when read forward and backward. One example is Gateman/Nametag.
- Create a second slide that includes some answers (optional):
    o   Lived/devil, drawer/reward, desserts/stressed, diaper/repaid
- Insert the slide into the beginning of the presentation if it is to be used as a soft opener. Then put up the slide prior to the webinar to help acclimate learners to the platform tools. If this is to be used as an opener, insert the slide at the start of the session. To use this as an energizer, insert the slide anywhere.

Trainer Process

- Put up the "Reversible Reflection" slide.
- Ask learners to place their guesses or ideas on the whiteboard.
- After 90 seconds, continue on to the next content piece if this is used as an energizer. If used as an opener, ask participants to make a connection between reversible words and what is being learned or will be learned.
  o Look for: discovering how words can be read both ways is like learning—learning is a discovery process; the content we are looking at is intentional just like we are looking for words that are intentional; humans have a need-to-know attitude and when searching for these words, we realize we really want to get the answer.

Producer Process

- Welcome participants as they enter the virtual room via text chat.
- Whiteboard an idea or two to spur thoughts.

Variations

- Create a list of just the first and last letter of the reversible word and see how many get filled in. Example: A_A, B_B, G_ _ _ _N, K_ _ _ K, D_ _ _ _ _ _ S and so on. Time it for 30-60 seconds for a quick energizer.
- Brainstorm only three-letter words for quicker reaction and response. For more advanced critical thinkers, limit responses to five letters or longer.
- Tie the word puzzle to the content whenever possible. Use the word puzzle to transition to a new topic.

Webinars with WOW Factor

WEBINAR LENGTH: Any
ACTIVITY LENGTH: 5 minutes
INSTRUCTOR SKILL LEVEL: Novice
PARTICIPANT SKILL LEVEL: Novice
SUPPLIES: Slide
TOOLS: Group Text Chat

CLOSER
LEARNING ACTIVITY
OPENER
SOFT OPENER
ENERGIZER
REVISITER

RIDDLE ME THIS

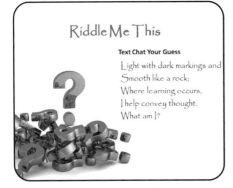

Purpose
Establish a Learning Community, Introduce New Concept, Refocus Learner

Setup
- Create a slide that says the following:
  - Light with dark markings and smooth like a rock, where learning occurs, I help convey thought. What am I?
  - Text chat your guess.
- Create a second slide that includes the answer: A whiteboard
- Create a slide that includes the following:
  - I am a source of communication. I am a way of meeting. I wink at you. I am known as the "Great Gossiper." I am intellectual. What am I?
- Create a second slide that includes the answer: A computer
- Insert the slides into the beginning of the presentation or as energizer slides in the middle of the slide deck.

Trainer Process

- Put up the "Riddle Me This" slide.
- Ask learners to text chat the answer or ideas as they come up with one.
- When someone has the right answer, move on to the next slide.
- When that has been solved, ask participants to make a connection between the riddles and what is being learned or will be learned.
  - Look for: tools we will use today; part of how we learn is by writing things down; sometimes we think we are being clear, but the learner may not grasp it
- No matter the riddle, it can be used as a quick way to energize a group and get brain cells firing again.

Producer Process

- Review answers to riddles and update leader's guide with possible responses that relate.

Variations

- Each learner is responsible for coming up with a riddle about a learning theme or topic covered. These need to be emailed to the facilitator prior to the next webinar (along with the answer). Use the "Riddles" throughout the next session to energize learners and revisit content in a fun way.
- Use easier riddles for quicker reaction and response. For more advanced critical thinkers, use slightly more complex riddles.
- Tie the riddle to the content whenever possible. Use riddles as a way to transition from one topic to another.

Webinars with WOW Factor

WEBINAR LENGTH: > 60 minutes
ACTIVITY LENGTH: 5-10 minutes
INSTRUCTOR SKILL LEVEL: Novice
PARTICIPANT SKILL LEVEL: Novice
SUPPLIES: Slide
TOOLS: Group Whiteboard

CLOSER
LEARNING ACTIVITY
OPENER
SOFT OPENER
ENERGIZER
REVISITER

SEEK AND SOLVE

Purpose
Brainstorm, Establish a Learning Community, Familiarizing, Introduce New Concept, Preview Material, Recall Background Knowledge, Recall Information—Existing Schemas, Revisit

Setup
- Create an "Objectives" slide that has a list of class objectives as defined by the facilitator.
- Create a "Seek and Solve" slide that has an image of a spyglass as a watermark and the words "seek" in the top left corner and "solve" in the top right corner. Place a vertical line running down the middle of the slide to break the slide evenly into halves.
- Insert the "Objectives" slide at the very beginning of the presentation.
- To use as an opener, insert the "Seek and Solve" slide into the presentation after any opening tool practice slides. To use as a closer, insert this as the last slide before a break or the end of the session.

Trainer Process
- Have the "Objectives" slide up as participants enter the virtual meeting room.
- When the "Seek and Solve" slide comes up, have each participant post a question they have about the topic that is about to be covered on the "Seek" portion of the slide.
- After each person posts a question, they will then begin reading the questions and look to answer or "Solve" other people's questions on the "Solve" side of the whiteboard.
- Several of the questions will be answered before formally beginning because of varying knowledge in the virtual room.
- As questions are solved, they are crossed off.
- Throughout the session, jump back to the "Seek and Solve" whiteboard and see if any of the other questions have been answered.
- Each time questions are answered, have learners again respond by writing the answer on the solved side and crossing it off.
- By the end of the session, all "Seeking" questions should be answered on the "Solved" side of the whiteboard.
- If this is being done as a closer, have learners write a question at the very beginning of the session. At the end of the session, close by looking at the slide again and having learners cross off their question if it was answered. If it isn't crossed off, take time to respond or identify a resource to further clarify.

Producer Process
- If a question has been answered, make sure it is crossed off.
- Capture participants' questions and answers on the whiteboard to add to a Frequently Asked Questions resource for the facilitator.

Variations
- If the platform allows for object movement, have learners simply drag the question for which they have an answer to the solved side and either text chat or verbally share the answer.
- If you are short on time or are working with novice users, have them type in their question and highlight or star the questions for which they have answers.

WEBINAR LENGTH: Any
ACTIVITY LENGTH: 1-5 minutes
INSTRUCTOR SKILL LEVEL: Novice
PARTICIPANT SKILL LEVEL: Novice
SUPPLIES: Slide
TOOLS: Polling

CLOSER
LEARNING ACTIVITY
OPENER
SOFT OPENER
ENERGIZER
REVISITER

SIGNAL SURVEY

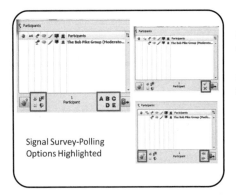

Signal Survey-Polling Options Highlighted

Purpose
Apply Material, Combining, Establish a Learning Community, Familiarizing, Innovate New Ideas, Introduce New Concept, Preview Material, Recall Background Knowledge, Recall Information—Existing Schemas, Refocus Learner, Revisit, Teach New Material

Setup
- Create a "Signal Survey" slide(s) that has a question and a small screenshot highlighting the polling tool or signal to be used. A signal could be a smiley face or learners could raise their hand or clap to show approval. Questions could relate to pacing, content, level of interest in the subject matter, true/false questions about prior knowledge, yes/no surveys, etc. Create as many question slides as needed.
- Become familiar with signals on the platform you will be using.
- Insert the slides as the first slide if used as an opener to get a pulse on where learners are at with the content. Insert throughout for revisiting or energizing and at any point when used as the learning activity.

Trainer Process

- Put up the "Signal Survey" slide.
- Share that learners will respond to several polling questions.
- Have learners stand up and stretch while they select their polling answer to the question.
- Turn on your webcam to demonstrate standing up and then model selecting an answer.
- Once everyone has selected their answer, post responses or talk through the overall reaction to the question.
- An example question might be "Is this process clear?" If you have multiple users frowning, you might poll the audience (see polling in chapter 5) and give them options for responding, or you may go deeper and provide an additional illustration to better clarify the process.

Producer Process

- Before questions go on the whiteboard, select the correct polling feature.
- Put up the polling results so all can view overall feedback.
- Assist learners with technical difficulties or questions.

Variations

- If you need a quick engager and haven't had a chance to prepare a slide, just add a whiteboard and insert a question in the moment.
- In you're in a time crunch, put up a timer for 2 minutes and have learners answer as many poll questions as possible.
- Have learners create their own poll questions by raising their hands and asking or writing on the whiteboard.
- Have participants work in breakout rooms to come up with a polling question that reviews the content covered, one per person. Once they are done, copy their questions into the main room and use as the polling questions.

Webinars with WOW Factor

WEBINAR LENGTH: Any
ACTIVITY LENGTH: 5-10 minutes
INSTRUCTOR SKILL LEVEL: Novice
PARTICIPANT SKILL LEVEL: Novice
SUPPLIES: Slide
TOOLS: Group Whiteboard

CLOSER
LEARNING ACTIVITY
OPENER
SOFT OPENER
ENERGIZER
REVISITER

SINGULARLY SPEAKING

Purpose
Apply Material, Brainstorm, Establish a Learning Community, Familiarizing, Introduce New Concept, Recall Background Knowledge, Recall Information—Existing Schemas, Refocus Learner, Teach New Material

Setup
- Create a slide that includes the following (these can be split into individual slides):
    o Title: Singularly Speaking
    o Image in the background of cattle or fish.
- Directions: Whiteboard words that either have no (or a rarely used) singular version. One example is cattle.
- Create a second slide that includes some answers (optional):
    o Agenda, braces, gold, gear, scissors, pants, trout, swine, fish, salmon, moose, deer, pike, sheep, aircraft, blues, cannon, stone, algae, data, graffiti, paparazzi, tings, pliers, billiards, measles, honesty.
- Insert the slide into the beginning of the presentation if this is to be used as a soft opener. Then put up the slide prior to the webinar to help acclimate learners to the platform tools. If this is to be used as an opener, insert the slide at the start of the session. To use this as an energizer, insert the slide anywhere.

Trainer Process

- Put up the "Singularly Speaking" slide.
- Ask learners to place their ideas on the whiteboard.
- After 90 seconds, continue to the next content piece if used as an energizer. If used as an opener, ask participants to make a connection between these types of words and what is being learned or will be learned. Have learners raise their hands and turn on their microphones to share.
    o Look for: only one way to do the process being learned; a lot of ideas when working and brainstorming in a group; team problem-solving goes quicker than doing alone

Producer Process

- Welcome participants as they enter the virtual room via text chat.
- Whiteboard an idea or two to spur thoughts.
- Turn on timer for 30-60 seconds (variation only).

Variations

- Create a slide with a lot of images. Each image must be the visual representation of a noun with no singular form like cattle, fish or algae.
- Use images or words only related to the content.
- Have learners work individually at first to come up with words and then, after 30-60 seconds, have them work together. Debrief with questions like: What helped you to be successful? What does success look like? What insights can we take away from this exercise and apply back at work?
- Tie the word puzzle to the content whenever possible. Use the word puzzle to transition to a new topic.

WEBINAR LENGTH: Any
ACTIVITY LENGTH: 1-5 minutes
INSTRUCTOR SKILL LEVEL: Novice
PARTICIPANT SKILL LEVEL: Novice
SUPPLIES: Slide
TOOLS: Group Text Chat

CLOSER
LEARNING ACTIVITY
OPENER
SOFT OPENER
ENERGIZER
REVISITER

SPORTSMANIA

Purpose
Establish a Learning Community, Refocus Learner

Setup
- Create a "Sportsmania" slide that includes the following:
  o Images of activities.
  o A selection of the following:
    - Shooting a jump shot
    - Running through tires
    - Batting a baseball
    - Serving a tennis ball
    - Skiing downhill
    - Spiking a volleyball
    - Swinging a golf club
    - Throwing a football
    - Juggling a soccer ball
    - Shooting an arrow
    - Shooting a hockey puck
    - Swimming underwater
    - Dunking a basketball
- Insert the slide anywhere throughout the presentation for fun as an energizer.

Trainer Process
- Put up the "Sportsmania" slide when learners are starting to fade.
- Have participants text chat their favorite sport to play or watch and one of the movements done in that sport.
- They can create their own or select one from the slide.
- Then announce that it's time for a "Sportsmania" break. Have them do the motion they chatted for 30-45 seconds to get their blood moving.
- Encourage participation by demonstrating the movements on a webcam.
- After the timer is done, ask participants to text chat how they are feeling now compared to before they took their sports break.

Producer Process
- Put up timer for 30-45 seconds.

Variations
- Put up the list on the screen and have participants change motions every 15 seconds for up to a minute.
- In need of a quick unplanned energizer? Put up a blank whiteboard and have learners post sports, and then get up and do that sport for 30 seconds. It is quick and easy to throw in at any time.

WEBINAR LENGTH: Any
ACTIVITY LENGTH: 2-5 minutes
INSTRUCTOR SKILL LEVEL: Novice
PARTICIPANT SKILL LEVEL: Novice
SUPPLIES: Stickers
TOOLS: Text Chat or Two-way Audio

CLOSER
LEARNING ACTIVITY
OPENER
SOFT OPENER
ENERGIZER
REVISITER

STICK IT

Purpose
Apply Material, Brainstorm, Combining, Familiarizing, Revisit

Setup
- Create a handout titled "Top Takeaways" for participants to write down learnings throughout the webinar.
- Prior to the webinar, send out a welcome package to your participants. Contents should include a welcome letter or confirmation and a page of stickers. The stickers can be colorful or as simple as dots.
- Create a "Stick It" slide that has an image of the sticker sheet with the page number of their "Top Takeaways" page.
- Insert the slide at whatever point needed for engagement or revisiting, or at the end if this is being used as a closer. This slide can be used multiple times during a session at various points.

Trainer Process
- Put up the "Stick It" slide.
- Have learners open their workbooks to their "Top Takeaways" page.
- Give 60 seconds to add two to three new learning ideas to their page. Allow a maximum of 60 seconds or you may lose them to email!
- After 60 seconds, have them sticker one idea they want to take action on right away.
- For a quick check to ensure they have found something, have participants text chat (or use two-way audio and share) their best idea.

Producer Process
- Mail materials and confirmation letter to learner prior to the session.
- Put up timer for 60 seconds.

Variations
- Have participants use a marker or highlighter instead of using stickers.
- Have learners raise their hands once they have added four ideas to their page so you know when they are ready to move on. If they have their hand up, they should also stand up and take a quick stretch break.
- When used as a closer, have everyone text chat or whiteboard their best idea.

WEBINAR LENGTH: Any
ACTIVITY LENGTH: 15 minutes
INSTRUCTOR SKILL LEVEL: Intermediate
PARTICIPANT SKILL LEVEL: Intermediate
SUPPLIES: Slide
TOOLS: Breakout Rooms, Group Whiteboard

CLOSER
LEARNING ACTIVITY
OPENER
SOFT OPENER
ENERGIZER
REVISITER

TEAM HUDDLE

Purpose
Apply Material, Brainstorm, Combining, Establish a Learning Community, Familiarizing, Innovate New Ideas, Introduce New Concept, Preview Material, Recall Background Knowledge, Recall Information—Existing Schemas, Refocus Learner, Revisit, Teach New Material

Setup
- Create a handout titled "Top Takeaways" for participants to write down learnings throughout the webinar.
- Create a slide that includes the following:
  o Title: Team Huddle
  o "Team moderator is the person with the most miles on their car"
  o "Task: Brainstorm top takeaways and highlight the group's top three takeaways [modify the task based on the purpose of the activity]."
- Insert the slide into the presentation partway through the webinar to revisit, before a break or at the very end as a closer, and anywhere throughout as needed for brainstorming, collecting new ideas, etc.

Trainer Process

- Have learners turn to their "Top Takeaways" page or the content page being worked on.
- Put up the "Team Huddle" slide.
- Share that groups will be put into breakout rooms in just a moment. If this is a closer, each group is to brainstorm concepts that have resonated with each person. If this is being used as a learning activity, have learners work together to accomplish the task.
- Have participants write these on their whiteboards using the webinar platform tools (different colors, drawing tools, text, etc.). Allow 3-4 minutes for this.
- The team moderator will stop the group when there is 1 minute left and have team members vote on the top three ideas brainstormed.
- Have all groups come back together, and the teams' moderators will share their whiteboard with the group. Any ideas that are duplicated do not need to be covered again.
- Have participants add to their "Top Takeaways" page in their workbooks while groups are sharing.

Producer Process

- Create breakout rooms.
- Post pre-made slide in breakout rooms with instructions.
- Put up a timer for 3-4 minutes and have it count down.
- Answer any questions that come through via text chat.
- Check in on breakout rooms and answer any questions.
- Post breakout room whiteboards in the main room for viewing or application share the whiteboards.

Variations

- With small groups, do this in the main room together.
- Have small groups focus on one topic area and brainstorm all key learning points from that section of content.

WEBINAR LENGTH: Any
ACTIVITY LENGTH: 1-5 minutes
INSTRUCTOR SKILL LEVEL: Novice
PARTICIPANT SKILL LEVEL: Novice
SUPPLIES: Pre-made Slide, Piece of Paper per Participant
TOOLS: Polling

CLOSER
LEARNING ACTIVITY
OPENER
SOFT OPENER
ENERGIZER
REVISITER

TRASH COLLECTOR

Purpose
Establishing a Learning Community, Refocus Learner

Setup
- Create a slide that includes the following:
    o   Title: Trash Collector
    o   An image of a garbage can or garbage truck in the background.
    o   List out the following:
        - Elbow and elbow
        - Foot and foot
        - Knee and knee
        - Forearm and elbow
        - Foot and elbow
        - Knee and elbow
        - Forehead and back of hand
        - Toe and finger
- Insert the slide anywhere throughout the presentation for fun as an energizer.

Trainer Process

- Put up the "Trash Collector" direction slide when learners start to fade.
- Have participants locate a piece of scrap paper and crumple it into a ball.
- Each participant stands up and locates a spot across the room or outside their cube. This spot becomes their imaginary trash can.
- Each person tries to toss their paper ball and hit their trash can.
- If they make the shot, they raise their virtual hand. They are "free" to pick up their garbage and sit back in their chair.
- If, however, they miss their garbage can, they get to collect their trash in one of the optional ways listed on the slide.
- Encourage participation by demonstrating the movements on a webcam.
- After everyone has retrieved their garbage, have learners use an emoticon or icon to show how they are feeling.

Producer Process

- Put on webcam and participate.
- Keep track of team points (variation only).

Variations

- Want competition? Split the learners into teams. Make teams fun—guys vs. gals, East Coast vs. West Coast, and so on. Do the trash collector energizer two to three times in a row with participants identifying new "trash cans" each time. If the learner makes the shot, they get one point. If the learner misses and collects the trash in the way the facilitator randomly selects, they get two points. Use this activity multiple times throughout the session; in the second half of the session, learners earn double points.
- Imagine the trash is really a treasure such as a wadded up deed to a house or a $20,000 check. Now retrieve it and smooth it out using one of the aforementioned ways.

WEBINAR LENGTH: Any
ACTIVITY LENGTH: 5-10 minutes
INSTRUCTOR SKILL LEVEL: Novice
PARTICIPANT SKILL LEVEL: Intermediate
SUPPLIES: Slide
TOOLS: Group Whiteboard, Group Text Chat

CLOSER
LEARNING ACTIVITY
OPENER
SOFT OPENER
ENERGIZER
REVISITER

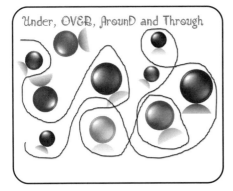

UNDER, OVER, AROUND AND THROUGH

Purpose
Recall Background Knowledge, Recall Information—Existing Schemas, Refocus Learner, Revisit

Setup
- Create an "Under, Over, Around and Through" slide that includes the following:
  o Multiple images of objects randomly placed with space between images. Place some of the images close together to increase difficulty of the activity. Images can be anything from products a company sells to fun, playful pictures.
  o Draw a line weaving up, down and all around the objects but not touching any of them.
- Insert the slide after content is covered to revisit or anywhere throughout for fun as an energizer.

Trainer Process

- Put up the "Under, Over, Around and Through" slide.
- Ask learners to use their drawing tools and move around the obstacles following the pre-made line denoting the path.
- The first person to make it through the obstacle course wins a small prize.
- If anyone "hits" or touches an obstacle along the way, they get to text chat one thing they have learned so far during the session (revisiter only).
- Demonstrate using a drawing tool and start the course. Purposely hit an object and text chat something learned.
- As comments are texted, read off what was written (revisiter only).

Producer Process

- Put up the timer (variation only).

Variations

- Put learners' names on the slide and associate each with a color; announce the race and who is in the lead as participants finagle their way through.
- Make it a race against time. Put up the slide a second time and see if learners can beat their original time.
- Leave out the pre-drawn line and have the facilitator draw the line in the moment while participants follow as quickly and accurately as possible.

WEBINAR LENGTH: Multiple Session
ACTIVITY LENGTH: 5 Minutes, Multiple Times
INSTRUCTOR SKILL LEVEL: Intermediate
PARTICIPANT SKILL LEVEL: Novice
SUPPLIES: Slide
TOOLS: Two-way Audio, Whiteboard

CLOSER
LEARNING ACTIVITY
OPENER
SOFT OPENER
ENERGIZER
REVISITER

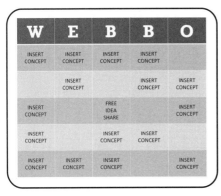

WEBB"O"

Purpose
Combining, Familiarizing, Introduce New Concept, Preview Material, Recall Background Knowledge, Recall Information—Existing Schemas, Refocus Learner, Revisit

Setup
- Create a "WEBBO" slide that has a sample WEBBO (bingo) card.
- Create a "WEBBO Words" slide that includes terms not already on the WEBBO board, which participants will use to fill in the empty spots on their card. Have more terms than blank spaces.
- Create a homemade WEBBO (bingo) card, which is a 5x5 grid. Fill 19 of the 25 spaces with concepts to be covered throughout the webinar sessions. The center space is a free space.
- Add printed WEBBO cards to your materials list to mail or email to participants prior to the session.
- Insert the slide at the beginning and throughout the session multiple times to remind the participants about the game.

Trainer Process

- Put up the "WEBBO Words" slide.
- As learners log into the session, have them fill in the blanks with ideas from the slide. One idea per blank.
- Give 2½ minutes for learners to fill in their blanks.
- Share the following WEBBO Rules:
  - As topics are covered, learners will cross off the topic and write one thing they learned about it in the proper box.
  - When a participant has completed the specified WEBBO pattern, such as five boxes in a row vertically, horizontally or diagonally, they raise their hand and text chat WEBBO.
  - Before receiving the prize, the learner must share one learning they had for each square in the winning pattern.
  - Before you continue on with new material, announce the next pattern for WEBBO. Other patterns can include four corners, the shape of a capital T or H, or blackout the board with every space covered. Insert the WEBBO card slide as the last slide to be used as the final closer.
- Prizes are awarded to each participant as they get WEBBO and share three or four of their blanks with the group.
- If this is being used as a closer, pair up the learners and have them share any three boxes they have filled in and what they learned in that content piece.

Producer Process

- Mail/email out WEBBO cards prior to the session.
- Put up timer for 2 1/2 minutes.
- Watch text chat for questions.
- Send out prizes awarded to participants after the session.

Variations

- The WEBBO card can be uploaded to the platform and downloaded and printed by each participant.
- To increase the challenge, create four versions with only 16 spaces pre-filled. Create a slide with the remaining terms and let participants choose in which boxes to place concepts.
- For a shorter webinar, play "WEB" and create a 3x3 grid with nine spaces.

WEBINAR LENGTH: Any
ACTIVITY LENGTH: 5 minutes
INSTRUCTOR SKILL LEVEL: Novice
PARTICIPANT SKILL LEVEL: Novice
SUPPLIES: Slide
TOOLS: Group Text Chat

CLOSER
LEARNING ACTIVITY
OPENER
SOFT OPENER
ENERGIZER
REVISITER

WHO DONE IT?

Purpose
Refocus Learner, Revisit

Setup
- Create a "Who Done It?" slide that has clues to a piece of content. Reveal one clue at a time if the platform allows for animation. If not, have clues prepared in advance and type them on the whiteboard one at a time. Prepare multiple clues and pilot test to ensure enough clues are created.
- Create additional slides if you're having learners guess multiple content areas. One slide per content or topic.
- Insert the slide(s) at whatever point needed for engagement and revisit or at the end if a closer.

Trainer Process
- Put up the "Who Done It" slide.
- Share that this is a game of sleuthing. Participants will need to grab their detective caps, pipes, and magnifying glasses to determine which piece of content or data was covered.

- Reveal information one click at a time about a given topic on the whiteboard. If this feature isn't available, just type in the clues.
- For ease, prepare the clues in advance in a word document and copy and paste them in to keep things moving.
- Participants watch the clues, both written and visual, and take guesses in the text chat area of the webinar.
- The first person to guess correctly wins a small prize or points that can be collected throughout the session.
- When someone has the right answer, move on to the next slide.
- Once learners have guessed the content, have each text chat one takeaway they have for that lesson. What will they try first? What was their biggest learning?

Producer Process

- Process winners and mail/email prizes as necessary.
- Watch text chatting area for correct answers.
- Create breakout rooms (variation only).
- Post the pre-made slide in breakout rooms with instructions (variation only).
- Put up a timer for 5-10 minutes and have it count down (variation only).
- Answer any questions that come through via text chat (variation only).
- Check in on breakout rooms and answer any questions (variation only).

Variations

- Have learners go into breakout rooms and create clues for a piece of content covered. Allow for 5-10 minutes for their discussion and brainstorming. When everyone is back in the main room, have each group reveal their clues one at a time and see how quickly others guess their topic.
- Give learners clues for being back on time from breaks or lunch. At the end of the session, use this as a closer. Those that have the additional clues will get the answer quicker, winning a small prize.

Webinars with WOW Factor

APPENDICES

APPENDIX A

Virtual Platforms

I hesitate to include this data in the grid because the second it is printed, its content will already be out-of-date; however, it will give you a starting point. Some platforms are more sophisticated and meant for teaching and training purposes, but are more difficult to learn, while others are very easy to begin using, but are light on the tools and capabilities. In the end, it is a matter of what is important to you and your team.

Name of platform	Adobe Connect	Webex	Gotowebinar	Zoom	Google Classroom	Google Meet	Blackboard Collaborate Ultra	Demio	Webinarjam	Webinar Ninja	Click Meeting	Any Meeting	Get Response	Microsoft Teams
Difficulty To Learn	3	3	1	1	2	1	2	1	2	1	2	2	3	3
Log On Difficulty	3	2	2	1	1	1	2	2	1	1	1	1	2	1
Download Required				X	X						X			
# Participants	1K	40K	3K	50K	1K	100	500	500	5K	1K	10K	1K	1K	20K
Access - Secured	X	X	X	X	X	X	X	X	X	X	X	X	X	X
Access - Open	X	X	X	X		X	X		X					X
Analytics	X	X	X		X		X	X	X	X	X	X		
Annotation Tools Participant	X	X	X	X	X		X	X			X		X	
Annotation Tools Presenter	X	X	X	X	X		X		X		X		X	
Application Sharing	X	X	X	X	X	X	X		X	X	X		X	X
Breakout Room - Whiteboard	X						X							
Breakout Rooms	X	X	X	X			X				X			X
Chat - Group	X	X	X	X	X	X	X	X	X	X	X	X	X	X
Chat - Private	X	X	X	X			X		X	X	X	X		
Chat - Producers	X						X		X					
Duplicate Webinar	X	X		X				X	X	X	X			X
Email Automation	X	X				X		X	X	X	X	X	X	X
Event Reminder	X	X	X		X			X	X	X	X	X	X	X
File Share	X	X	X	X	X	X	X	X	X				X	X
Free Trial/Version	X	X	X	X	X	X	X	X	X	X	X	X	X	
In Platform Video Share	X	X						X	X	X	X		X	X
In Platform Music Share	X								X		X			X
Integrated With Calendar	X	X			X	X				X			X	X
Mobile App	X	X	X	X	X	X	X	X	X	X		X	X	X
Multiple Presenters	X	X		X					X	X	X		X	
Polls	X	X	X	X			X	X	X	X	X	X	X	
Pricing	$$$	$$	$$$	$$	$	$	$$$	$	$	$	$	$$	$$$	$
Producer Control Tools	X	X	X	X			X		X		X	X		X
Q&A	X	X				X	X		X	X				
Quiz	X		X								X	X	X	
Recording	X	X	X	X	X	X	X	X	X	X	X	X	X	X
Screen Share	X	X	X	X	X	X	X	X	X	X	X	X	X	X
Timer	X			X										
Whiteboard	X	X	X	X	X		X		X		X		X	X

APPENDIX B

DOs and DON'Ts of Learning Champions

DO	DON'T
Talk about the webinar training with staff: what it will do for the company, what impact it will have, next steps for learning.	Feel like you have to be a subject matter expert. Just know where to go to find the answers.
Focus your attention on a few influential team members. Meet one-on-one to help motivate them and encourage their support of the training. Ask for their support.	Guess at the answers.
Find co-champions. They can be just as effective at speeding up the change or learning process. Support them and reward them with encouragement and praise.	Hesitate to ask for advice or help.
Involve all and make them aware of what the champion is there for.	Be a one-person show. Collaborate with other champions to see what they are doing.
Wear a shirt following the training that makes it easy for them to see who to ask for help. It may mean wearing the same shirt for three days.	Forget food and treats. These make feedback sessions far more enjoyable.
Invite others to give feedback and ask questions about the training. Provide support and alleviate concerns by troubleshooting and directing them to the answers.	Be intimidated by how much work being a champion can be. A champion might invest 30-60 minutes a day focusing on this aspect of the job.
Host feedback sessions. Share learnings and how the new knowledge is being used. Make topics fun: "Secret Shortcut Keys Identified."	Skip getting feedback from those implementing the webinar content.
Recognize staff who embrace the learning. Be sincere.	Keep learnings to yourself. Share with other champions, trainers and management.
Publicize results.	Forget or hide results because it didn't go perfectly.

APPENDIX C

Additional Resources

BOOKS

ASTD Handbook, 2nd Edition
Elaine Biech, ASTD Press, 2014.

A Trainers' Guide to PowerPoint
Mike Parkinson, ATD, 2018.

Creative Training: A Train-the-Trainer Field Guide
Becky Pike Pluth, Creative Training Productions, 2016

Design for How People Learn 2nd Edition
Julie Dirksen, New Riders, 2015.

Elearning by Design
William Horton, Pfeiffer, 2006.

E-learning Basics: An Info-line Collection
ASTD Editors, ASTD Press, 2012.

Engaging Modern Learners
Jennifer Hofmann, Amazon, 2018.

Kirkpatrick's Four Levels of Training Evaluation
Donald L. Kirkpatrick, Donald L. Kirkpatrick, ATD, 2016.

Live and Online!: Tips, Techniques and Ready-to-Use Activities for the Virtual Classroom
Jennifer Hofmann, Pfeiffer, 2004.

Producing Virtual Training, Meetings, and Webinars
Kassy LaBorie, ATD, 2020

The State of Virtual Training 2020 by Cindy Huggett
https://www.cindyhuggett.com/blog/2020sovt/

The Trainer's Balanced Scorecard
Ajay M. Pangarkar and Teresa Kirkwood, Pfeiffer, 2009.

The Trainers Handbook Updated Edition
Karen Lawson, Pfeiffer, 2021.

WEBSITES

These links include information about training and development ranging from elearning to classroom training. All links were active at printing, but can break or be terminated at any time as they are not owned by Creative Training Productions. These sites are for informational purposes and do not reflect endorsement.

- **BobPikeGroup.com**
  The Bob Pike Group
  Provides training workshops and consulting services for both classroom and online training.

- **BrandonHall.com**
  Brandon Hall Research
  Provides useful elearning and distance learning information.

- **Canva.com**
  canva
  Canva is a graphic design platform used to create powerful presentations, social media graphics, posters, documents and other visual content. The platform is free to use but offers paid subscriptions as well.

- **DaveBirss.com/storydice/**
  The classic story ideas generator is now free online. With over 50 options for each die, this is a great tool for interactivity and engagement.

- **Edu-Games.org**
  Make your own word or sudoku game or choose one of the saved puzzles.

- **flippity.net**
  flippity
  Easily turn a Google™ spreadsheet into a set of online flashcards and other cool stuff.

- **FreeMind.sourceforge.net**
  FreeMind
  FreeMind is a free mind-mapping software written in Java.

- **Horton.com**
  William Horton Consulting, Inc.
  Elearning design specialists with a wealth of industry knowledge and resources.

- **Masie.com**
  Masie Center
  Home of the Learning Consortium, the Masie Center is an international think tank dedicated to exploring the intersection of learning and technology.

- **Videomaker.Simpleshow.com**
  Simpleshow Video Maker
  Explainer videos rule! And now creating them is a piece of cake! With MySimpleshow, you can develop and create your own professional illustration video. There are both free and fee-based versions.

- **Pixabay.com**
  Pixabay GmbH
  Pixabay is a website for sharing photos, illustrations, vector graphics, film footage and music, exclusively under the custom Pixabay License and is free to use.

- **PuzzleMaker.com**
  Discovery Education
  Puzzlemaker is a puzzle generation tool for teachers, students and parents. Create and print customized word search, criss-cross, math puzzles, and more using your own word lists.

- **Qwizdom.com**
  Qwizdom, Inc
  This company provides interactive data-gathering solutions for corporations, schools and government agencies around the world. Qwizdom offers an advanced radio-frequency audience response technology where everyone in the room participates and provides instant feedback to the presenter.

- **Soapboxify.com**
  Endurance Learning
  Soapbox is an online tool that allows you to create virtual training sessions and face-to-face training presentations with accompanying materials (facilitator guide, PowerPoint slides, handout templates) in as little as 10 minutes.

- **TD.org**
  Association for Talent Development (ATD)
  The world's largest association dedicated to workplace learning and performance professionals. ATD's members come from more than 120 countries. Members work in thousands of organizations of all sizes, in government, as independent consultants and suppliers.

- **TurningTechnologies.com**
  Turning Technologies
  TurningPoint audience response system integrates 100 percent into Microsoft® PowerPoint® and allows audiences and students to participate in presentations or lectures by submitting responses to interactive questions using a ResponseCard® keypad or other hand-held/computer devices.

- **UMU.com**
  UMU
  UMU's interactive platform allows you to engage and interact with participants via their mobile devices and project the responses in real time. With UMU, (which stands for You, Me, Us) everyone participates, so you can accurately gauge your audience and identify common interest topics.

APPENDIX D

Gaining Management Support for Training

1. Form a steering committee or task force. Typically this is only done if the training you design is widescale. If it's just a one-hour webinar, this is unnecessary.
2. Involve the decision-makers in the decisions that happen prior to design, and include them in high-level communications throughout the project.
3. Prove the value of investing in training. Show how teaching online is a cost savings as well as a time savings. Typically training online takes half the time of what we do face-to-face and doesn't require travel time or expense.
4. Anchor your needs assessment and training to the company's strategic plan. Familiarize yourself with these plans prior to meeting with management so they can easily see how it relates to real needs.
5. Design training to meet perceived needs as well as real ones. For example, your client may ask you to design a session on closing the sale, but if your needs assessment uncovers that the real need is actually overcoming objections, fold both into the equation.
6. Set clear goals and expectations, then deliver what you promise. Under-promising and over-delivering is far better than not meeting expectations. It is very easy for scope creep to occur and derail the original goals for the session. If managers ask that additional content be included, pause and ask everyone if that should be a separate webinar.
7. Prioritize for importance and check for relevance. It's important to allow learners to connect the learning to their positions and make it relevant for themselves.
8. Evaluate results. Adjust, edit, re-design if necessary. Be accountable. Assure that learning is transferred back onto the job.
9. Share reports with stakeholders. People like to feel "in" on things. From the very beginning, determine who needs to be on the stakeholder list so no one is left out.
10. Publicize your own successes. Get testimonials from influential people. If this step gets missed, it can be detrimental to the next project. When management hears and sees great results on one webinar, it is much easier to get buy-in on the next one.

APPENDIX E

Stakeholder Engagement for Learning Solution

Stakeholder Names	Support Level					Reasons for Rating	Resistance P-Personal loss B-Belief C-Cultural	Reason for Resistance	Influence Strategy			
	Strongly Against	Moderately Against	Neutral	Moderately Supportive	Strongly Supportive				Who	What	When	

Source of Resistance	Definition of Source of Resistance
Personal Loss	People fear loss of security, money, power, influence, decision making autority. May lack skills & resources to change. Habit, fear of the unknown/failure, predisposition to change, power struggles, turf, relationships
Belief	People believe the change is unneccessary; not confident change will succeed and/or organiztion lacks the resources to implement the change. If it's not broken, don't fix it...
Cultural	People resist because it is different from "how we do things around here." Old cultural mindsets, traditions and/or group relationships.

Approaches to Resistance

Facilitation	The best approach to creating change is to work with people to help them achieve goals that also reach to the goals of the change project (win-win). This is a good practice when people want to collaborate but are struggling to adjust to the situation and achieve the goals of change.
Education	When people are not really bought into the rationale for the change, they may well come around once they realize why the change is needed and what is needed of them. In particular, if new skills are required, you can provide these via a focused course of education.
Involvement	When people are not involved physically or interllectually, they are unlikely to be involved emotionally either. One of the best methods of getting people bought in is to get them involved. When their hands are dirty, they realize that dirt is not bad, after all. They also need to justify their involvement to themselves and so persuade themselves that is the right thing to do.
Negotiation	When the other person cannot easily be persuaded, then you may need to give in order to get. Sit them down and ask what they are seeking. Find out what they want and what they will never accept. Work out a mutually agreeable solution that works just for them and just for you.

APPENDIX F

ADDIE Model Overview for Webinars

	ANALYZE	DESIGN
TACTICS	Spending time with the client to transfer knowledge and ask key questions such as: • Who is the audience? • What webinar experience do they have? • What do they need to learn? • What constraints exist? • What is the timeline for project completion? • What other systems or best methods will this change impact? • How do we define "success"?	Building a blueprint of the training program. • Defining learning objectives • Determining course content • Determining instructional strategies and methods • Determining the evaluation approach • Documenting resource requirements (e.g. funding, time, personnel, equipment, etc.)
MEETING EXAMPLES	• Process Flow • Business Scenario/ Use Case • Business User Reviews • Usability Labs • Needs Assessment Interviews	• Course outline review • Training design review
% OF TIME NEEDED	25%	20%

DEVELOP	IMPLEMENT	EVALUATE
The actual "construction" of elements that will support the training program. • Course materials • Learning activities • Lesson plan and trainer's guide • Tests or other assessment materials • Job aids	The point at which the training plan is finally developed and delivered. This plan consists of: • "Dry Run" webinar (e.g. pilot) • Updates and revisions to the webinar training following the dry run • Finalization of training • Train-the-trainer sessions (if needed) • Roll out the live webinar course	Systemic process that determines the quality and effectiveness of the training as well as the final product. • Did we meet our objectives? • Did the learning experience add value? • Like It (Level 1): Assesses the participants' initial reactions to the training course. • Learn It (Level 2): Assesses the amount of information that participants learned. • Use It (Level 3): Assesses whether or not the participant was able to transfer the learning and apply on the job (6 weeks to 6 months post-training). • Impact (Level 4): Assesses the financial impact of the training course related to ROI (6 months to 2 years post-training).
• Periodic content-review meetings	• Dry-run webinar • Final logistics-review meeting(s) • Final content-review meeting(s) • Live webinar session	• Pilot/Roll out feedback sessions • Roll out postmortem • Post-training feedback development and update
35%	15%	5%

APPENDIX G

Before, During, and After Checklist

BEFORE THE SESSION	DURING THE SESSION	AFTER THE SESSION
• Prepare thoroughly • Be familiar with the software • Know your content • Create strong objectives • Prepare to teach in the online medium • Create closers, openers, revisiters and energizers • Have a backup plan • Experience it as a participant • Follow the four Ps – plan, prepare, practice, perform • Select captains or champions for the training • Assess your audience • Create active learning activities • Host a pre-elearning session to make sure trainees know how to log on and be successful with the interface	• Start and end on time • Open the e-meeting room early • Provide printed handbooks for learners to work in • Give and receive feedback • Correct learners effectively • Allow/plan for silence • Problems will arise, be flexible • Stay organized • Engage your audience • Have a subject matter expert (sme) in the room • Have two computers running so you can also log in as a student • Plan for revisit and reuse	• Follow up with participants on parking lot items • Bridge the content gap with an email or voicemail • Provide it support for users • Enhance the content and curriculum • Hold a postmortem with key stakeholders to share successes and learnings

**Webinar interactive activities can be done using the following tools: whiteboard, quizzes, polling, text chat, application sharing, webcam, VoIP, breakout rooms, recordings, videos and asynchronous games.

APPENDIX H

Objectives Term List

How will you know if participants have learned your training material? Before the class is designed, define the learning objectives of the course using words that are measurable. "Understand," "know," and "learn" are not measurable. A well-written objective identifies the audience, the behavior, what conditions exist and to what degree the behavior will be mastered. Following are many verbs you can use that will help you write measurable objectives so you can easily gauge if your learning goals were met.

Examples of performance verbs include:

Knowledge						
acquire	define	indicate	point	recite	select	tell
cite	distinguish	label	quote	recognize	show	trace
collect	draw	list	read	relate	state	write
count	identify	name	recall	repeat	tabulate	
Comprehension						
associate	contrast	distinguish	examine	interpret	predict	restate
classify	describe	explain	express	interpolate	report	review
compare	differentiate	estimate	illustrate	locate	represent	translate
compute	discuss					
Application						
apply	demonstrate	generalize	modify	prepare	review	solve
accelerate	dramatize	illustrate	operate	practice	schedule	translate
calculate	employ	interpret	order	relate	sequence	use
change	examine	interpolate	plan	report	show	utilize
complete	experiment	locate	predict	restate	sketch	
Anaysis						
analyze	connect	detect	divide	explain	order	
appraise	contrast	diagram	estimate	infer	question	
classify	criticize	differentiate	examine	inspect	separate	
compare	debate	distinguish	experiment	inventory	summarize	
Synthesis						
arrange	combine	create	formulate	invent	organize	produce
assemble	compose	design	generalize	manage	plan	propose
collect	construct	detect	integrate	modify	prepare	rewrite
Evaluation						
appraise	convince	decide	grade	rate	select	
assess	critique	discriminate	judge	recommend	support	
choose	criticize	estimate	measure	revise	test	
conclude	determine	evaluate	rank	score		
AVOID using these words or phrases as they are too general and are NOT measurable.						
appreciate	be familiar	grasp the	have	know	realize	think
be aware of	with	significance	knowledge of	learn	remember	understand
				perceive	study	

APPENDIX I

Tasks Required to Design, Produce and Deliver a Participant-Centered Webinar Checklist

CHECKLIST	TEAM MEMBER RESPONSIBLE	DUE DATE	DONE	N/A
Analysis				
Identify knowledge, skills, attitudes				
Draft needs assessment				
Administer assessment				
Analyze assessment data				
Determine depth of knowledge needed				
Webinar Objectives				
Write business objective				
Write manager objective				
Write learner objective				
Define project scope				
Write session description				
Course Setup				
Identify/purchase webinar platform				
Create invitation link				
Secure conference bridge number/VoIP				
Set pilot date/time				
Set roll out date/time				
Select trainer				
Select producer				
Select champions or captains				
Evaluation				
Determine level 1-4 (Kirkpatrick) evaluation criteria				
Write objectives for module 1				
Write objectives for module 2				
Write objectives for module 3				
Write objectives for module 4				

CHECKLIST	TEAM MEMBER RESPONSIBLE	DUE DATE	DONE	N/A
Write objectives for module 5				
Write objectives for module 6				
Design Session				
Brainstorm content				
Chunk content				
Schedule physical break every 60-90 minutes				
Identify webinar tools available				
Create job aids				
Define and create pre-work				
Select or develop soft openers, openers and closers				
Select or develop energizers and revisit activities				
Identify and develop follow-up materials				
Select additional media to use: music/video/articles				
Determine breakout rooms/ groups				
Develop all components** for module 1				
Develop all components**for module 2				
Develop all components** for module 3				
Develop all components** for module 4				
Develop all components** for module 5				
Develop all components** for module 6				

CHECKLIST	TEAM MEMBER RESPONSIBLE	DUE DATE	DONE	N/A
Develop leader's guide with producer notes				
Create games and exercises housed online for asynchronous use				
Develop a backup plan for activities				
Create level 1 session evaluation				
Design slide deck content				
Create handouts/learner workbook				
Draft registration information				
Identify participant download				
Develop participant packing list for mailing (email/post)				
Purchase supplies/materials for session and mailing				
Develop mailings/invitations • Welcome letter • Platform instructions with session link • Supplies for session • Pre-work assignments				
Production/Layout				
Complete layout of slides				
Complete production of video clips				
Complete production of audio clips				
Complete layout of leader's guide				
Complete layout of handouts				
Create PDF of all participant materials				

CHECKLIST	TEAM MEMBER RESPONSIBLE	DUE DATE	DONE	N/A
Communication				
Send mailings/invitations				
Send invitation reminder				
Review class roster				
Send out follow-up materials after session				
Practice				
Examine all content				
Practice all tools on platform				
Record practice and review				
Experience session as a learner				
Make revisions to session				
Support				
Verify IT support				
Reserve second computer				
Producer practice session				
Contact information for conference call/webinar platform				
Print webinar platform FAQ and quick-reference guides				

APPENDIX J

Design Templates

Webinar Session Name: ©2021 Creative Training Productions

ID	**Description**	**Scope** / **Trainer**	**Webinar Information** Invitation Link: Conference Bridge Number: Date: Time:
Objectives	**Business Objective**	**Learner Objective**	**Manager Objective**
Team	**Trainer Role**	**Producer Role** / **Learner Role**	**Production** PPT: Slides: Websites to visit:
Resources	**Materials** Pre-work: Mailings: Handouts: Slides: Whiteboard Activities: Video: Audio Bridge: Documents:	**Content Expert Resources** / **Follow Up Contact Information**	**Product Information** Tools: Programs: Platform Contact:

Webinars with WOW Factor

Webinar Session Planning Checklist

Webinar Title: _____ **Trainer:** _____ **General Description:** _____

©2021 Creative Training Productions

Session Info

Administration

Registration
- ☐ Invitation Sent
- ☐ Online
- ☐ Phone
- ☐ Internal
- ☐ Paper
- ☐ Recorded Session

Billing
- ☐ Free
- ☐ Cost Center # _____
- ☐ Per Learner
- ☐ Per Session
- ☐ _____
- ☐ _____

Documents Used
- ☐ Handouts
- ☐ Activity Log
- ☐ Polling Questions
- ☐ Recorded Session
- ☐ Feedback Forms
- ☐ Tests
- ☐ Quizzes

Security
- ☐ Open Session
- ☐ Closed Session
- ☐ Guest Invitations

Follow-up
- ☐ Completion Email
- ☐ Certificate
- ☐ _____
- ☐ _____
- ☐ _____
- ☐ _____

Communication

E-mail
- ☐ Trainer to Learner
- ☐ Learner to Learner
- ☐ Platform to Learner
- ☐ Invitation
- ☐ Invitation
- ☐ Reminder
- ☐ Handouts

Mailings
- ☐ Welcome Letter
- ☐ Instructions
- ☐ Handouts
- ☐ Supplies for Session
- ☐ Assignments

Web-Conference Tools
- ☐ Text Chat
- ☐ Audio Conference
- ☐ Bridge
- ☐ VoIP
- ☐ Whiteboard
- ☐ _____
- ☐ _____

- ☐ Breakouts
- ☐ Application Sharing
- ☐ Polling
- ☐ Video Conference
- ☐ Web Hunt

Webinar Features and Plans

Assessments
- ☐ Polling
- ☐ Yes/No
- ☐ Multiple Choice A-C
- ☐ Multiple Choice A-D
- ☐ Multiple Choice A-E
- ☐ Speed
- ☐ Pre-test
- ☐ Post-test

Evaluation
- ☐ Pre-test
- ☐ Post-test
- ☐ _____
- ☐ Session Feedback
- ☐ 30/60/90 Day
- ☐ Follow-up

Course Announcements
- ☐ Session Announcement
- ☐ Session Description
- ☐ Session Objectives
- ☐ Registration Information
- ☐ Technical Requirements for Computer
- ☐ About the Trainer

Support
- ☐ Producer
- ☐ FAQ checklist
- ☐ Leader's Guide
- ☐ Second Computer

Test
- ☐ Platform
- ☐ Slides
- ☐ Hyperlinks
- ☐ Websites

Resources
- ☐ Books
- ☐ Terms
- ☐ Downloads
- ☐ Handouts

NOTES:

Webinar Session Activity Planner

©2021 Creative Training Productions

Session Info

Webinar Title:

Trainer

Activity Information

General Description

Whiteboard Slide or Application Screenshot

Activity Directions

Time	Group Size	Materials Needed	Resources	NOTES:

APPENDIX K

Sample Evaluation Questions and Scales

General Instructor/Producer Questions
Scale—Strongly Agree, Somewhat Agree, Neutral, Somewhat Disagree, Strongly Disagree
- The instructor demonstrated knowledge of content
- The instructor effectively managed the classroom (e.g. set clear expectations, kept class on task, covered all materials, etc.)
- The producer effectively managed the online platform (e.g. transitions to breakout rooms, application sharing, technical support)
- The instructor created a comfortable learning environment (e.g., open to questions, responsive, etc.)
- The instructor adapted learning styles to meet individuals' needs
- The instructor delivered materials at an appropriate pace
- The instructor was knowledgeable about the materials
- The instructor followed through on commitments (e.g., follow-up items, parking lot questions, etc.)

Scale—Very Good, Good, Average, Fair, Poor
- Rate the effectiveness of the instructor

General Materials Questions
Scale—Strongly Agree, Somewhat Agree, Neutral, Somewhat Disagree, Strongly Disagree
- The materials were (insert any of the following terms: engaging, professional in appearance, current, well-organized, appropriate length, thorough, appropriately challenging, etc.)
- There was an adequate balance of lecture and activity
- The activities were appropriate for meeting the objectives
- Examples helped me better understand concepts presented in class (e.g., calls, scenarios, mock calls, etc.)

Scale—Open Ended
- Overall additional comments or suggestions about the materials
- Overall additional comments or suggestions about the instructor

General Review/Assessment Questions

Scale—Strongly Agree, Somewhat Agree, Neutral, Somewhat Disagree, Strongly Disagree

- The webinar environment was conducive to learning
- I was able to use computer resources when necessary (e.g., IT/producer was available, there were enough computers, systems were accessible)
- Practice time was effective
- There was adequate review time throughout the training
- The review activities were helpful

Scale—Extremely Satisfied, Somewhat Satisfied, Neutral, Somewhat Dissatisfied, Extremely Dissatisfied

- How satisfied were you with the training session

APPENDIX L

Checklist for Co-Facilitation

Prior to the Session
_ Individually prepare by reviewing the session to analyze:
    _ The session objectives
    _ The objectives of each module
    _ The key points and activities for each module
_ Schedule ample time for planning either in person or on the phone
_ Take some time to get to know each other
_ Discuss each other's style of planning and facilitating
_ Take time to discuss your views about the session topic and come to a common understanding on:
    _ Key objectives of each module
    _ Key points to cover in each module
    _ The process or adult learning methods used in each module
    _ Problems encountered facilitating the course before and how to avoid them
    _ How you will divide your tasks and roles (fairly)
_ Examine areas of disagreement
_ Discuss any concerns about potential challenges that participants may present
_ Review each other's triggers
_ Discuss how to best interject a thought if not on 'stage'
_ Decide how to keep track of time and a discreet signal to use with one another to reference time
_ Strategize about how to stick to the original outline and how to transition
_ List what should be prepared in advance and who will do it
_ List what materials need to be mailed to participants or downloaded during the session and who will do it
_ Agree on a log-in time for the session for set up and check-in before the session begins
_ Schedule time after the workshop to debrief
_ Review each other's triggers
_ Discuss what each of you will do while the other is taking the lead

in facilitating. This could include observing the dynamics in the room, text chatting responses to questions, getting ready for your next section, etc.
_ Agree not to contradict, interrupt or correct one another in front of the participants. Find a time during break or when participants are working on an exercise to raise questions or concerns with your co-facilitator.

Dealing with Difficult ... Co-Trainers!
_ Be mindful of your differences and take them into account in developing your co-facilitating plan
_ Differences include:
    _ Sector of the union or geographic region
    _ Gender
    _ Race
    _ Education
    _ Experience
_ Discuss how you will respond if participants start to favor one of the facilitators because of these differences
_ Honestly discuss your strengths and weaknesses in facilitating this session
_ Decide how to support each other to take advantage of your respective strengths and to improve or overcome your respective weaknesses

During the Session
_ Trust and respect each other as equal partners
_ Know your roles and responsibilities and follow through
_ Check in with one another throughout the session
_ Support one another
_ Listen to your co-facilitator and the workshop participants even when you're not "on"
_ Help each other keep on schedule
_ Check in at breaks to see how things are going, how your co-facilitator is feeling and whether any adjustments need to be made
_ Be flexible
_ Learn from your co-facilitator's style
_ Use private text chatting

- Assert yourself if your co-facilitator is talking too much
- Remember that it is okay to make mistakes
- Take the initiative to step in if your co-facilitator misses an opportunity to address something
- If not facilitating, act as a participant
- Leverage the strength of styles, presentation and facilitation energy

After the Session
- Listen carefully to one another's self-evaluation before giving feedback
- Discuss what worked well
- Examine what did not work
- Brainstorm what could have been done differently
- Be honest and respectful of each other as equal partners in co-facilitating when providing feedback, especially if you feel there were problems
- Use written evaluations as a reference point to talk about the session, and assess your effectiveness as co-facilitators
- Realize the importance and potential difficulty of debriefing a challenging workshop

APPENDIX M

Best Practice Back-Up Plans for Tech Failures

Possible Problems	Best Practice Solutions
Lack of technology	Pre-work, send materials
Loss of audio	Wait, have back-up conference call line
VoIP lag time for some learners	Have a teleconference bridge ready
Lack of participation	Use small groups, keep things moving, use polling features to assess pace, use team leaders
Technical difficulties	Have support person online, have a producer to troubleshoot with individuals so you can stay focused
Materials don't arrive	Create PDFs prior to mailing and email to participants
Confusing or abstract topic	Do pre-planning and have some pre-work for learners to gain familiarity with topic
Lag time	Allow for it ... be willing to pause, have independent work available for learners to work on
Do not understand the materials	Ask questions to ensure comprehension, have other facilitators and learners preview materials and give feedback to prevent
Network goes down	Take a 15-minute break, even if a break just occurred; have everyone log back in at a specified time, pre-plan a date/time for a make-up session
Phones go down	Text chat to everyone and take a 15-minute break so IT can work on solution
Handouts won't download	Have a PDF version and email
Slower learners	Use a producer to assist those people

APPENDIX N

Synchronous Glossary

Annotate—During a webinar when trainer, producer or participant use drawing or text tools on the whiteboard.

Application Sharing—Participants view instructor's documents and applications. Facilitators can also request permission to view a participant's computer applications and desktop.

Asynchronous Learning—Learning done alone with no time or location restraints. Available 24/7. A self-paced program typically done with a mobile device or computer.

Bandwidth—Speed of data transfer via network or modem using the internet. The greater the bandwidth the faster the computer reads information and gets it to the end user.

Breakout Sessions—Tool used to create subgroups in a webinar much like a small group discussion in a classroom or meeting. Learners can go in and connect with a few participants and then be returned to the main room and rejoin the large group.

Closer—An activity that ties things together and revisits the content.

Computer-Based Learning – Computer-aided learning (CD-ROM or online via the internet).

eLearning—The use of information and computer technologies to create learning experiences.

Energizer—An activity that helps get blood flowing and brains thinking. Best used when energy is low. Does not have to be relevant to the content.

Evaluation—A feedback form that allows for a trainer to collect information and assess the session content, materials, trainer and participant-engagement levels. Some are done using polling features, some are digital and automatically tabulated and others are produced in a paper-pencil fashion.

Hyperlinks—A function that allows a user to click the link and be placed in another section of a document or web page.

Internet—Usually the world wide web, but can also be email and file sharing.

Intranet—Hosted by a company for its internal use. Not accessible to the public, although it can contain links to the internet.

Learning Activity—An interaction that allows the facilitator to teach as the activity progresses. It takes the place of a lecture.

Opener—An activity that encourages networking and breaks preoccupation. An opener is relevant to the content; in this way, it is different from an icebreaker.

Pacing—Feature that helps instructors know if their speed of content delivery is too fast or slow.

Playback—Allows for the webinar session to be recorded and reviewed at a later date.

Polling—A synchronous tool that allows for answering questions using polling buttons. Questions come in the form of yes/no, true/false, multiple choice and short answer. Other quick ways to poll are to use emoticons, hand raising and other icons that vary from one webinar platform to another.

Revisiter—A revisit is when the learner interacts with content already covered. A review is when the facilitator interacts with content already covered.

Soft Opener—This activity engages the audience, sets the tone, puts the attendees at ease, and allows learners to practice using platform tools before the official start of the webinar. It is relevant to the content.

Text Chat—Real-time conversation between participants and instructor that is done by text. Text chat is in most platforms and can be programmed to allow private chatting or only public chatting.

Two-Way Audio—Any means by which individuals can talk to one another whether it is via the internet or a conference call bridge. In one-way audio, only the trainer can speak.

Video Conference—A live teleconference conducted via television equipment or desktop computer via a network or webinar platform.

VoIP—Digitally sending the voice over the internet. Stands for 'Voice over Internet Protocol.'

Webcam—A digital camera capable of sharing live video feed and images over the internet or webinar platform.

Whiteboard—Tool used in webinars to share content, materials and information in real-time with others. Most allow for annotation and can be modified in the moment. All learners can view the whiteboard.

Webinars with WOW Factor

INDEX

			Type of Interaction						Tools Required						
	Name	Page	C	L	O	S	E	R	Group Text Chat	2-way Audio	Group White-board	White-board	Break Out Rooms	App Share	Poll
Applying Material	BRAVO!	110	x	x	x	x	x	x		x				x	
	Bursting Balloons	112	x			x		x			x		x		
	Card Match	114		x				x		x		x			
	Check and Balance	120	x	x							x		x		
	Chit Chat	122		x			x	x	x						
	Find and Fix	126	x	x							x		x		
	Gallery Recognition	134	x		x	x		x	x						
	Group Work	136		x					x	x			x		
	Heart Smart	138					x								x
	I Object	140	x						x	x			x		x
	OOHHRAH Cheer	156					x	x		x					x
	Pop Quiz	162	x	x	x			x							x
	Pop Ups	164		x			x	x	x						x
	Quick Questions	168	x					x				x			
	Raptivity	170	x	x	x	x	x			x				x	
	Signal Survey	178		x	x		x	x							x
	Singularly Speaking	180	x	x	x	x	x	x	x	x	x	x	x	x	x
	Stick It	184	x			x	x	x	x	x					
	Team Huddle	186						x			x		x		
Brainstorm	Around the World	106	x	x	x			x			x	x			
	ATZRR	108	x		x			x			x				
	BRAVO!	110	x	x	x	x	x	x		x				x	
	Bursting Balloons	112	x	x				x			x		x		
	Chart Chase	116	x					x			x				
	Chart Chase 2	118	x					x				x			
	Chit Chat	122		x			x	x	x						
	Find and Fix	126	x	x				x		x	x				
	Group Work	136		x					x	x			x		
	Heart Smart	138					x								x
	I Object	140		x					x	x			x		
	Literary Assumptions	148	x	x	x	x	x			x					
	Map It	150			x	x	x		x	x					
	Pop Ups	164		x			x	x	x						x
	Q it Up	166	x		x	x	x					x			
	Seek and Solve	176	x		x					x					
	Singularly Speaking	180	x	x	x	x	x			x					
	Stick It	184	x			x	x	x	x	x					
	Team Huddle	186	x	x				x						x	
Combining	BRAVO!	110	x	x	x	x	x	x		x				x	
	Bursting Balloons	112	x	x				x			x		x		
	Check and Balance	120	x	x						x		x			
	Find and Fix	126	x	x					x		x				
	Flow Chart Fill-in	128	x	x	x		x			x	x				
	Gallery Recognition	134	x		x	x		x	x						
	Group Work	136		x					x	x		x			
	Heart Smart	138					x								x
	I Object	140		x					x	x			x		
	OOHHRAH Cheer	156					x	x	x						x
	Pop Quiz	162	x	x	x			x							x
	Pop Ups	164		x			x	x	x						x
	Signal Survey	178	x	x	x		x	x		x	x	x	x	x	x
	Stick It	184	x				x	x	x	x					
	Team Huddle	186	x	x				x						x	
	Webb"O"	192	x		x		x	x			x	x			

Section	Name	Page	C	L	O	S	E	R	Group Text Chat	2-way Audio	Group White-board	White-board	Break Out Rooms	App Share	Poll
Establishing a Learning Community	ATZRR	108	x		x			x				x			
	BRAVO!	110	x	x	x	x	x	x			x			x	
	Bursting Balloons	112	x		x			x			x		x		
	Chart Chase	116	x					x			x				
	Chart Chase 2	118	x					x				x			
	Double Trouble	124			x	x	x				x				
	Group Work	136		x					x	x			x		
	Heart Smart	138					x								x
	I Object	140		x						x	x		x		
	Literary Assumptions	148	x	x	x	x	x				x				
	Map It!	150			x	x	x		x		x		x		
	Mastermind Mix	152			x		x			x			x		
	Pass It On-UNO™ Style	158					x					x			
	Pesky Palindromes	160			x	x	x		x						x
	Pop Ups	164		x			x	x							x
	Reversible Reflection	172			x	x	x		x						
	Riddle Me This	174			x	x	x								
	Seek and Solve	176	x		x			x			x				
	Singularly Speaking	180	x	x	x	x	x				x				
	Sportsmania	182					x		x						
	Team Huddle	186	x	x				x			x		x		
	Trash Collector	188					x								x
Familiarizing	ATZRR	108	x		x			x				x			
	BRAVO!	110	x	x	x	x	x	x			x			x	
	Bursting Balloons	112	x		x			x			x		x		
	Chart Chase	116	x					x			x				
	Chart Chase 2	118	x					x				x			
	Chit Chat	122		x			x	x	x						
	Find and Fix	126	x	x					x	x					
	Flow Chart Fill-In	128	x	x	x			x			x	x			
	Frozen Acronyms	130	x		x	x		x							x
	Gallery Recognition	134		x			x	x							
	Group Work	136		x					x	x			x		
	I Object	140		x						x	x		x		
	Identification Shuffle	142	x	x	x		x				x				
	Interactive Crossword	144	x	x	x	x	x	x							x
	Interactive Word Search	146	x	x	x	x	x		x						x
	Literary Assumptions	148	x	x	x	x	x				x				
	Pop Quiz	162	x	x	x										x
	Singularly Speaking	180	x	x	x	x	x				x				
Innovating New Ideas	BRAVO!	110	x	x	x	x	x	x			x			x	
	Bursting Balloons	112	x		x			x			x		x		
	Chart Chase	116	x					x			x				
	Chart Chase 2	118	x					x				x			
	Chit Chat	122		x			x	x	x						
	Group Work	136		x					x	x			x		
	Heart Smart	138					x								x
	I Object	140		x						x	x		x		
	Pop Ups	164		x			x	x							x
	Team Huddle	186	x	x				x			x		x		

Webinars with WOW Factor

	Name	Page	Type of Interaction						Tools Required						
			C	L	O	S	E	R	Group Text Chat	2-way Audio	Group Whiteboard	Whiteboard	Break Out Rooms	App Share	Poll
Introduce New Concept	BRAVO!	110	x	x	x	x	x	x		x				x	
	Chit Chat	122		x			x	x	x						
	Double Trouble	124			x	x	x				x				
	Find and Fix	126	x	x					x		x				
	Frozen Acronyms	130	x		x	x		x							x
	Gallery Recognition	134		x			x	x	x						
	I Object	140		x						x	x		x		
	Identification Shuffle	142	x	x	x			x			x				
	Interactive Crossword	144	x	x	x	x	x	x	x						x
	Interactive Word Search	146	x	x	x	x	x	x	x						x
	Literary Assumptions	148	x	x	x						x				
	Map It!	150		x	x	x			x		x		x		
	Mastermind Mix	152		x						x		x			
	Pesky Palindromes	160		x	x	x			x						x
	Pop Quiz	162	x	x	x			x							x
	Pop Ups	164		x			x	x							x
	Q it Up	166	x		x	x					x				
	Reversible Reflection	172		x	x	x			x						
	Riddle Me This	174		x	x	x			x						
	Seek and Solve	176	x		x			x			x				
	Singularly Speaking	180	x	x	x	x	x	x			x				
	Team Huddle	186	x	x				x			x		x		
	Webb"O"	192	x		x		x	x	x			x			
Previewing Material	BRAVO!	110	x	x	x	x	x	x	x				x		
	Bursting Balloons	112	x		x			x			x		x		
	Card Match	114		x				x	x		x	x			
	Flow Chart Fill-In	128	x	x	x			x			x	x			
	Fulfilling Fill-in-the-Blank	130		x	x	x	x					x			
	I Object	140		x						x	x		x		
	Identification Shuffle	142	x	x	x			x			x				
	Interactive Crossword	144	x	x	x	x	x	x	x						x
	Interactive Word Search	146	x	x	x	x	x	x	x						x
	Literary Assumptions	148	x	x	x	x	x								
	Pop Quiz	162	x	x	x			x							x
	Pop Ups	164		x			x	x							x
	Seek and Solve	176	x		x			x			x				
	Team Huddle	186	x	x				x			x		x		
	Webb"O"	192	x		x		x	x	x			x			
Recall Background Knowledge	ATZRR	108	x		x			x			x				
	BRAVO!	110	x	x	x	x	x	x	x				x		
	Bursting Balloons	112	x		x			x			x		x		
	Card Match	114		x				x	x		x	x			
	Chart Chase	116	x					x			x				
	Chart Chase 2	118	x					x				x			
	Chit Chat	122		x			x	x	x						
	Find and Fix	126	x	x				x	x		x				
	Flow Chart Fill-In	128	x	x	x			x		x	x				
	Frozen Acronyms	130	x		x	x		x							x
	Gallery Recognition	134		x			x	x	x						
	Group Work	136		x					x		x		x		
	Heart Smart	138					x								x
	Identification Shuffle	142	x	x	x			x			x				
	Interactive Crossword	144	x	x	x	x	x	x	x						x
	Literary Assumptions	148	x	x	x	x	x				x				x
	Pop Quiz	162	x	x	x			x							x
	Singularly Speaking	180	x	x	x	x	x	x			x				
	Under, Over, Around ...	190					x	x		x					

Becky Pike Pluth, M.Ed., CSP

	Name	Page	Type of Interaction						Tools Required						
			C	L	O	S	E	R	Group Text Chat	2-way Audio	Group White-board	White-board	Break Out Rooms	App Share	Poll
Recall Information-Existing Schemas	ATZRR	108	x		x			x			x				
	BRAVO!	110	x	x	x	x	x	x	x					x	
	Bursting Balloons	112	x		x			x		x		x			
	Card Match	114		x				x	x		x				
	Find and Fix	126	x	x					x	x					
	Flow Chart Fill-In	128	x	x	x			x	x		x				
	Frozen Acronyms	130	x		x	x		x							x
	Gallery Recognition	134		x			x	x							
	Group Work	136		x					x	x		x			
	Heart Smart	138					x								x
	I Object	140		x						x	x	x			
	Identification Shuffle	142	x	x	x			x			x				
	Literary Assumptions	148	x	x	x	x					x				
	Pop Quiz	162	x	x	x			x							x
	Pop Ups	164		x			x								x
	Seek and Solve	178	x		x			x			x				
	Singularly Speaking	182	x	x	x	x	x				x				
	Under, Over, Around ...	192					x	x	x						
Refocus Learner	ATZRR	108	x		x			x			x				
	BRAVO!	110	x	x	x	x	x	x	x					x	
	Bursting Balloons	112	x		x			x		x		x			
	Chart Chase	116	x					x			x				
	Chart Chase 2	118	x					x				x			
	Chit Chat	122		x			x	x	x						
	Double Trouble	124		x	x	x				x					
	Flow Chart Fill-In	128	x	x	x			x	x		x				
	Gallery Recognition	134		x			x	x	x						
	Heart Smart	138					x								x
	I Object	140		x						x	x	x			
	Interactive Crossword	144	x	x	x	x	x	x	x						
	Interactive Word Search	146	x	x	x	x	x	x	x						
	Literary Assumptions	148	x	x	x	x					x				
	One and Done Break	154					x						x		
	Pesky Palindromes	160		x	x	x			x						
	Pop Quiz	162	x	x	x			x							x
	Reversible Reflection	172		x	x	x			x						
	Singularly Speaking	180	x	x	x	x	x				x				
	Under, Over, Around ...	190					x	x	x						
	Who Done It?	194	x				x	x	x						
Review	ATZRR	108	x		x			x			x				
	BRAVO!	110	x	x	x	x	x	x	x					x	
	Bursting Balloons	112	x		x			x	x		x		x		
	Card Match	114		x				x	x		x				
	Chart Chase	116	x					x			x				
	Chart Chase 2	118	x					x				x			
	Chit Chat	122		x			x	x	x						
	Flow Chart Fill-In	128	x	x	x			x	x	x					
	Frozen Acronyms	130	x		x	x		x							x
	Gallery Recognition	134		x			x	x							
	Group Work	136		x					x	x		x			
	Heart Smart	138					x								x
	I Object	140		x						x	x	x			
	Identification Shuffle	142	x	x	x			x			x				
	Pop Quiz	162	x	x	x			x							x
	Under, Over, Around ...	190	x				x	x	x						
	Who Done It?	194	x				x	x	x						
New Material	BRAVO!	110	x	x	x	x	x	x	x					x	
	Flow Chart Fill-In	128	x	x	x			x	x		x				
	Frozen Acronyms	130	x		x	x		x							x
	Group Work	136		x					x	x		x			
	Heart Smart	138					x								x
	I Object	140		x						x	x	x			
	Identification Shuffle	142	x	x	x			x			x				
	Literary Assumptions	148	x	x	x	x					x				
	Pop Quiz	162	x	x	x			x						x	
	Pop Ups	164		x			x	x							x
	Singularly Speaking	180	x	x	x	x	x				x				
	Team Huddle	186	x	x				x			x		x		

About The Author

Becky Pike Pluth is not your typical speaker. Over the past 18 years, Becky has designed and delivered more than 5,000 interactive webinars on a variety of topics including sales, customer service, train-the-trainer, performance consulting, and virtual presentation skills. Her in-person sessions at *Training Magazine* and Association for Talent Development conferences have drawn standing-room-only audiences for the last fourteen years. She regularly has more than 2,000 registrants for her free webinars for The Bob Pike Group and *Training Magazine* Network. Becky has more than 24 years of experience in training delivery and design and business operations, and she has been the owner of The Bob Pike Group for the past eight years. She also is the author of *Creative Training: A Train-the-Trainer Field Guide, 101 Movie Clips that Teach and Train* and nine other influential books and resources.

In designing these interactive webinar tools, Becky has utilized sustainable change and adult learning principles. These methods are practical, repeatable, and highly effective. A trained educator, Becky expanded into corporate training after completing her master's degree in teaching and learning. She also is a Certified Speaking Professional through the National Speakers Association.

Other Titles by Becky Pike Pluth

CORE Series
Closers, Openers, Revisiters, and Energizers

Each of the titles in this series is filled with dozens of activities to help you increase content retention to at least 80 percent! Close with action planning, open with impact, revisit content creatively, and energize learners to keep them refreshed and attentive.

The techniques, tips, and activities in all books have been tested in the crucible of real training situations and will work for you, too!

CORE 3 for Face-to-Face Training *CORE 4 for Technical Training*
SCORE 5 for Webinar Training *SCORE 6 for One-on-One Training*

Training Difficult People

Training brings with it a variety of challenges, including difficult behaviors in learners which can quickly derail your class.

To keep your training moving forward, equip yourself with more than 270 tactics to help either turn around those reluctant learners—like the latecomers, texters, or know-it-alls—or mitigate the effects of ongoing negative behavior for other participants.

Each of the 23 learner types has its own section for easy and immediate reference so you can use it for your own just-in-time training.

101 Movie Clips that Teach and Train

Using short clips from movies can relay learning points more dramatically and quickly than any lecture. Let *101 Movie Clips that Teach & Train* jumpstart your creativity for lesson planning or training design by providing you with the perfect movie clip for more than 100 topics, including discrimination, leadership, team building and sales. Each clip referenced comes with cueing times, plot summary, scene context and cogent discussion questions. All topics are cross-referenced so you can easily find the perfect clip for your teaching or training needs.

Secrets of a Powerful Presentation

Rich Meiss, Priscilla Shumway and Becky Pike Pluth are decorated presenters with nearly a century of experience between them. In this book, they share their planning steps for organizing a presentation, tips for effective visuals that work with your presentation, not against it, and best practices for presenting with impact.

Creative Training: A Train-the-Trainer Field Guide

Becky Pike Pluth has combined decades of personal training experience with excellent brain research about how to train easily, successfully, and effectively. She makes sure the reader understands the important, brain-based reasons for using ILPC (Instructor-Led, Participant-Centered) training strategies. Even better, Becky adds her own delightful stories and sense of humor as she shows you how to teach in ways the human brain learns best. This book is a "must" for any trainer's bookshelf!

Other Media

Webinars with Wow Factor Ready-To-Go Slides

Quick-start your next interactive webinar with well-designed PowerPoint slides! The slides that accompany the interactivities in chapter 13 are available for you to use in your next online training. There are 60 slides in all to give your session that WOW factor!

Ordering information for these can be found at
https://store.bobpikegroup.com/books/.
To order by phone, call 800-383-9210.

Engineer Curiosity

Virtual Train-the-Trainer Courses from The Bob Pike Group

Interactive Virtual Trainer

Experience how virtual training can be just as engaging and effective as classroom training when it's participant-centered.

Learn how to engage your webinar audience right from the start. You only have four minutes to hold your audience's attention during a webinar. After that, minds start to drift and attention fades.

In this live online workshop (three 3-hour sessions), you'll explore the practical application of Creative Training Techniques® in webinar design and delivery.

Virtual Presentation Skills Crash Course

The skills you need to present like a pro to virtual audiences with ease!

Like it or not, you are judged not only on what you say, but how you say it. And right now, there's the extra pressure of presenting your ideas virtually. Online meetings, trainings, and pitches challenge even seasoned presenters because of technology and distance.

Where should you look while presenting? How do you involve people from start to finish? Should the camera be on you very long? What do you need to do differently online?

How to Quickly Convert Classroom Teaching to Live Online Training Crash Course

When training moves online, the rules change. You only have four minutes to hold learners' attention—after that minds wander. One hour of classroom training doesn't translate to one hour online. Designing for training online presents new tools and new limitations to factor into every project. All this change just as people are maxed out on screen time more than ever before.

Get the basics of virtual design—everything you need to know to quickly convert classroom content for online delivery. This crash course is for designers and trainers who want to convert or create programs that will be 3 hours in duration or less. This is a three-hour virtual workshop.

> *For more information on these or other train-the-trainer sessions, go to:*
> **www.bobpikegroup.com/public-and-onsite-train-the-trainer-courses**